Architectural
GUIDE
To CAMBRIDGE And EAST ANGLIA
Since 1920

Charles McKean

Cover Design: James H Forbes
Book Design: J H Forbes and Charles McKean
Maps: Mark Potter, Peter and Liz Holmes
Grotesques: Liz Holmes

New Town Material: Courtesy of the
New Towns themselves

Letchworth Trail: Mervyn Miller

This publication received assistance from the
Arts Council of Great Britain

ERA Publications Board
RIBA Eastern Region

© Charles McKean 1982

Printed by Lindsay & Co Ltd, Edinburgh

Architecture is lowered to the level of its utilitarian purposes: Boudoirs, WCs, radiators, ferro-concrete, vaults or pointed arches etc, etc. This is construction, this is not architecture. Architecture only exists when there is a poetic emotion.

Le Corbusier
(translated by Frederick Etchells)

The Seven Crutches of Modern Architecture

'The most important crutch in recent times is not valid now: **the Crutch of History.** In the old days you could always rely on books.

The Crutch of Pretty Drawing: it's a wonderful crutch because you can give yourself the illusion that you are creating architecture while you're making pretty drawings. Architecture is something you build and put together.

The Crutch of Utility: they say a building is good architecture if it works. Merely that a building works is not sufficient. You expect that it works. If the business of getting the house to run well takes precedence over your artistic invention the result won't be architecture at all: merely an assemblage of useful parts.

The Crutch of Comfort: after all, what is architecture for but the comforts of the people living there? But when that is made into a crutch for doing architecture, environmental control starts to replace architecture.

The Crutch of Cheapness: anybody that can build a $25,000 house has indeed reason to be proud, but is he talking about architecture or his economic ability?

The Crutch of Serving the Client: serving the client is one thing, the art of architecture is another.

The Crutch of Structure: structure is a very dangerous thing to cling to. You can be led to believe that clear structure clearly expressed will end up being architecture by itself. You say "I don't have to design any more. All I have to do is make a clear structural order."

I like Corbusier's definition of architecture. The play of forms under the light. And, my friends, that's all it is. You can embellish architecture by putting the toilets in. But there was great architecture before the toilet was invented. . . .' (*Abridged.*)

From a talk by American Critic and architect Philip Johnson to Harvard students in 1954.

INTRODUCTION

This guide has been designed as a work of architectural topography for Eastern England, drawing attention to some of the more important buildings constructed in that area since 1920. Topography has been defined as 'architectural humour', and so it may be in this case. However, the intention of this guide is to act as a sign-post, and to indicate to those unaware of the architectural history, or the geography of this part of England, where to find these more interesting buildings and what they are likely to find once they arrive.

The buildings featured in this book illustrate the changing pattern of patronage since 1920, both as it specifically affected East Anglia, and also as East Anglia affected Britain as a whole. The influence of Letchworth Garden City, founded in 1909, still persisted when the First World War ended, and East Anglia was in the throes of the Arts and Crafts. Barry Parker, besides building in Letchworth, was involved in housing at St Neots and the Hospital in Royston; and Baillie Scott, a late Arts and Crafts architect, designed a number of houses in Cambridge. Elsewhere in the region, the mood was traditional or neo-Georgian exemplified by the buildings of Sir Edwin Lutyens, Sir Giles Gilbert Scott and Sir Herbert Baker.

Being part of the Home Counties, however, the area was soon exposed to modern architecture; the earliest of which made its appearance at Silver End in Essex by Sir John Burnet and Partners. This highly innovative and continentally inspired workers' village was followed by a rash of houses in South Hertfordshire built for *avant-garde* London commuters and in Cambridge for similarly minded academics at the University. The influence of the film and aircraft industries in Hertfordshire together with the rapid developments along the new main roads encouraged those trends.

Admittedly, some of the grander excitements of the '30s passed the region by: only one Connell Ward and Lucas house — and not one of their most successful; only one Wallis Gilbert factory and an indifferent one at that; the seaside development at Frinton lacks the sparkle of those at Skegness and Bexhill; and few of the great 1930s cinemas. By contrast, the region contains the country's two Garden Cities and buildings by Wells Coates, Christopher Nicholson, Lubetkin and Tecton, Maxwell Fry, Burnet Tait and Lorne and Murray Easton. Moreover, for those interested in older buildings, an intriguing collection of buildings by Sir Edwin Lutyens can be found in Knebworth, with which he had a family connection (St Martin's Church, Golf Clubhouse, Homewood, 2 Deards End Lane and three sets of cottages); and by C F A Voysey in Chorleywood and Bushey (**The Orchard**, Shire Lane, Chorleywood 1901; **Sunnybank** (adjacent) 1904; **Tilehurst**, Grange Road, Bushey 1903; **Avalon** also Grange Road and **Myhollme**, Merryhill Road, all in Bushey).

By the early '30s, there was a real battle of styles. The definition of a modern house was reduced to the

3

simple statement of a flat roof. A pitched roof on the same dwelling removed its distinction (as H C Hughes found in Cambridge); conversely a flat roof on an otherwise ordinary house was supposed to lend it style.

John Betjeman in a speech (July 1932) reflected as follows: *now we come to the architectural chaos — which is today's when class distinctions have broken down, together with the distinction of English architecture. We have Sir Reginald Blomfield and Sir Herbert Baker visibly building in the monumental Queen Anne style. We have the Architectural Association going crazy over Sweden. Meanwhile, in the Cotswolds, gentlefolk are weaving and spinning, fighting a losing battle with a machine, painting finger bowls with flower designs, and dribbling paint over earthenware jars in a mistaken zeal for the old Morris Movement. Meanwhile some of the more high spirited people who call themselves tradionalists, but who are really Bolshevist Spies trying to ruin our tastes with sham Queen Anne and the like, have now had a try at what they think is modern. I always know them because they call their efforts 'jazz modern'. A few lines jaggered here and there, an absence of curves, a meaningless boggle at proportions, and the few staring colour contrasts and the job is done — quicker and cheaper than Queen Anne.* It would be wrong to suggest that such sporadic and isolated developments in any way constituted a general trend before the Second World War. When Norwich came to re-build its city hall in the 1930s, the style adopted was that of what might be called *Scandinavian Modern;* an elongated version of stripped down, neo-Georgian with a Swedish tower.

By 1939, British house architecture, so the magazines thought, was achieving a new vernacular-brick, pitched roofs and perhaps an asymetrical balcony. The influence of the War made itself felt in mass production, low-cost buildings which were refined for military purposes — military camps, hospitals, training centres and the like. The War was followed by several years' severe rationing of building materials — so much so that the construction of anything at all was something of an achievement. It became an end in itself. Thus the sad little book *The New Small House* (Architectural Press, 1953) has examples of new houses whose principal claim for attention is their very existence. For the most part, they have pitched roofs, brick or boarded walls, the very occasional arched window and remarkably little incidental delight. Much the same can be said for most 1950s buildings in Eastern England. Their stylistic traces of the Festival of Britain — windows boxed out in shallow concrete frames, spindly porch roofs, canted metal balconies and pale brick were added to the pre-war inheritance of metal windows in strips. A great deal of the resultant legacy is clumsy, ugly and undistinguished. The trouble, as can clearly be seen in the Bank of England works in Debden was that the details were too insignificant to have any accumulative effect on bulk; no contrast, no flowing lines, no character and no delight.

After the end of building licensing in the early 1950s, Eastern England saw a building boom which it had never experienced before in its history and is never likely to again. In addition to the four New Towns, there was a tremendous expansion to collegiate Cambridge, and the creation of two totally new Universities. The preponderance of modern buildings in this book is a direct reflection of the relative quantities of building over the decades. The types of buildings for which architects were commissioned changed dramatically. In the 1930s, the dominant building types were private houses, factories, town halls and hospitals. Between 1953 and 1960 occurred the first major boom in school building. In 1957, a decade of grand University and College building began. In 1960, or thereabouts, town centre and office redevelopments became predominant. By 1972, that had faded. In its place is housing for special needs and old people; fire and police stations; more town halls and civic centres; factories, infill and rehabilitation. Throughout the post-war period, housing in mega — and other — structures persisted as a major building type. Private houses appeared less frequently; in their place, schools, hospitals, old people's homes, libraries, swimming pools, and the entire paraphernalia of the Welfare State. The investment in social benefit between 1956 and 1976 is probably unparalleled in the country's history, and whatever its architectural merits, the achievement is visible in built form. In some cases, architects had to deal with new forms for new types of buildings; but they also had to deal with an increasingly remote client who governed his patronage by an ever growing system of rules and regulations. It is one thing to design a building for a single individual with strong tastes and views. It is quite another to design one for a Committee which frequently does not have direct access to finance, but has to borrow it from others who may themselves have views on the design.

The advent of these complicating factors coincided with the prevalent view that buildings should be designed as sculptures in space; they had to be able to be seen in the round, so that architectural prowlers could study them from all angles to ensure that the honesty of the facade was reproduced in the rear. The result was the partial destruction of the street scene and the historic characters of towns and villages. With some notable exceptions, that pattern lasted for a number of years, and architects lost the touch of designing places instead of individual buildings. The damage caused by that process — perhaps symbolised by the pathetic Tudor Gateway standing isolated in the back yard of the telephone building in Norwich — was being learnt towards the end of the 1960s. The sense of place was taking the upper hand in the public's affection over the design of individual buildings. Now, to judge from what is being constructed at the moment, the public is looking for total anonymity in architecture, always as long as it provides a familiar backdrop of brick walls and tiled or slated roofs. Thatch would undoubtedly be insisted upon were it not so difficult and expensive.

5

Conclusions

The individual Modern Movement buildings of the 1930s stood out as jewels in an otherwise traditional and often sombre environment. They achieved their effect by contrast. However, when the style of architecture became the norm, the contrast was lost and the architectural experience became more arid. The future of good architecture in the Eastern Counties will depend upon the realisation of the value of contrast. In the midst of all this neo-traditional building, architects and planners should have the courage to encourage skilful and exciting, modern buildings. As in the 1930s, they would enhance rather than detract from their surroundings. Whether or not the buildings featured in this guide will justify such an optimistic conclusion is up to the reader to decide.

It is by accident rather than design that this book has turned into an examination of styles. One major conclusion from the exercise is that most buildings of modern architecture can be dated with as precise a stylistic accuracy as any buildings in the past. There are very few exceptions.

Sources

The vast majority of the buildings in this book have been unearthed and visited by the team of people credited in *acknowledgements*. However, for the older buildings, considerable reliance has been placed on a number of written sources. In addition to the normal help available from the technical magazines, credit must be given to the following:

First and foremost to Sir Nikolaus Pevsner and his achievement of County architectural topographies in his *Buildings of England* series. Specific mention might be made of Bridget Cherry's second edition of the Hertfordshire volume.

Modern Homes in Britain, 1919-1939, by Jeremy Gould, and published by the Society of Architectural Historians (1977). It should be noted that Gould's definition of a modern house was that its common characteristic was a flat roof.

Twentieth Century Houses, Raymond McGrath (Faber & Faber, 1934).

The Modern House in England, F R S Yorke (1948).

The New Small House, F R S Yorke and Penelope Whiting (Architectural Press, 1953).

The Architect and Building News. A late lamented journal whose architectural coverage between the Wars was particularly helpful.

Architecture in Hertfordshire, 1929-79. An exhibition guide of good value published by the Hertfordshire Association of Architects.

Cambridge New Architecture. Edited by Nicholas Taylor (1971).

ERA. Journal of the RIBA Eastern Region (1968-1975).

Villages of Vision, Gillian Darley (Architectural Press, 1976).

Acknowledgements

This book was conceived under the aegis of the Publications Board of the RIBA Eastern Region whose Chairman, Patricia Stewart, has nursed it through difficult times. In addition to the help received from architect and building owners, the information gathering was primarily carried out by a group of architects chaired by David Thurlow. These were:

Anthony Cleary, Michael Innes, James Cornish, Mark Potter, Hans Fleck, Graham Beighton, Brian Hayward, Russ Craig, Percy Mark, John Manning, Tom Wilkinson, Graham Walker, Colin Huggins, Mervyn Miller, Reg Curtis, Douglas Chalk, David White, David Charles.

Thanks must also go to Keith Miller, Tony Hucklesby, Jo Robotham, Essex County Council, Gillian Darley, Wilfred Court, and Tony Hales. Bill Allen gave first-hand help on Welwyn; and Tom Jestico and Dean Hawkes kindly read through the preliminary text. Peter Melvin provided constant support. Derek Plummer searched journals.

The RIBA supported this book, and particular credit goes to Shirley Matthews for her administration; also to Sheila Rosser, Tina Wotherspoon and Tayona McKeown for their typing. The benevolent acquiescence of the Royal Incorporation of Architects in Scotland and its long-suffering staff in this strange foreign endeavour is to be recognised. The Master and Fellows of Christ's College Cambridge kindly gave permission to reproduce the Gropius drawing. The photograph of The Whipsnade Elephant House is by permission of the Zoological Society of London.

Mark Potter deserves special thanks for the thoroughness of his Cambridge investigation, for the maps, and for his magical mystery tour to find lost buildings throughout the region. Similar thanks go to James Cornish for his discoveries in Norfolk, and to David Charles in Essex. Peter and Liz Holmes were particularly helpful in completing the maps, and adding the grotesques.

Sponsors

We should also like to thank those sponsors of this publication, without whose help there would have been no book.

New Towns Commission, Norwich City Council, Stevenage New Town, Essex County Council, Basildon New Town, Bush Builders, Harlow New Town, R G Carter Ltd, Peterborough New Town, William Sindall Ltd, W G Neville Ltd, Coulsons Ltd, London Brick, Messrs Fairclough Ltd, Ibstock Bricks.

Last but not least, thanks must go to the Arts Council of Great Britain which first promised help toward this project over four years ago, and still kept its word.

The result of the total sponsorship is that the cover price of this guide is just over one-third of what it would have had to be without it.

A Note on the credits

Throughout the book, buildings produced by Local Authority Architects' departments have identified the architects' departments and the job architects where possible. The name of the Chief Architect officer has not been included, so as to avoid tedious repetition. However, the ability of the job architect to realise a fine building is often contingent upon the quality of his Chief Officer to make that possible, and the quality of the Chief Officer in choosing the right architect in the first place. We would wish to pay tribute therefore to the Chief Officer of the various Local Authorities in the area in question throughout these periods. Those whose buildings are included in this book are as follows:

Cambridge City: G C Logie I M Purdy J M Milner.

Cambridge County: H H Dunn S E Urwin W H Wingate R H Crompton P R Arthur.

Huntingdon and Peterborough County: H Leete T H Longstaffe S J Hands S M Holloway K G Sparrow.

Bedfordshire County: S C Jury V S Goodman J C Barker N M White.

Hertfordshire County: C H Aslin G C Fardell J Digby J Onslow.

Essex County: F Whitmore, G Topham Forest, J Stuart, H Conolly, R Crowe, A J Willis.

East Suffolk County: C G Stillman E J Symcox E J Cundliffe H G Tuffley.

West Suffolk County: A A Hunt J Creese J Digby J Brian Jackson.

New Suffolk County: J Brian Jackson.

Norfolk County: C J Norton C H Thurston G C Haydon K J King J F Tucker.

Norwich City: W H Town J N Meredith L G Hannaford D E Percival C Heathcote J H Pogson A C Whitwood.

Photographic Credits

Where no credit for a photograph is given, the photograph originated from the architect's office. Virtually all the photographs are those selected by the architects themselves who kindly absorbed the reproduction fee. The names of the photographers are otherwise credited alongside each photograph.

Sir Nikolaus Pevsner

The judgements of Sir Nikolaus Pevsner are reprinted from the relevant volumes of the *Buildings of England* series by permission of Penguin Books Ltd.

Grotesques

The following architects may be recognised among Liz Holmes' grotesques: Wells Coates, Professor Sir Albert Richardson, Terry Farrell, David Thurlow, Colin St John Wilson, Nicholas Grimshaw, Eric Lyons, Richard Rogers, David Roberts, Sir Frederick Gibberd, Maxwell Fry, Baillie Scott, Sir Edwin Lutyens, Sir Leslie Martin, Norman Foster, Quinlan Terry, and James Stirling.

Organisation of this book

The original intention was to organise the book on an historical basis: that is, buildings were to be included in date order. As other gazeteers have discovered before, such an arrangement may make a good architectural history, but it makes a dreadful architectural guide.

The book is therefore organised on a combination of both. Buildings are arranged first, on a county basis; and then an alphabetical basis of towns and villages within these counties. Cambridge, Norwich and Ipswich are so significant in their own counties that they are placed at the beginning of the counties.

In each location, the buildings are listed in date sequence although only in Cambridge does some historical perspective really appear.

Although over 400 buildings have been selected from over 1,000, it is acknowledged that there must be many other good examples which have escaped the trawl. They are listed in three categories: important buildings which require a photograph and relatively lengthy description; interesting buildings worth a detour if you are in the vicinity, some of which are illustrated; and finally those that are worth a glance in passing.

In most cases, the building is given with its address, the architectural office or practice (the job architect or designer(s) in brackets) the date of completion and, in some cases, the contractor or builder.

Where such information is missing, that may be attributed either to poor records, or to the stated architects' office's unwillingness to release the relevant information. That is particularly so of the 'job architect', and the addresses of some of the more private of secure buildings.

Important Note: Accessibility

Although many of the buildings are accessible to visitors, or are visible from the public highway, as many are privately owned and occupied. Users of this guide are asked to respect that privacy.

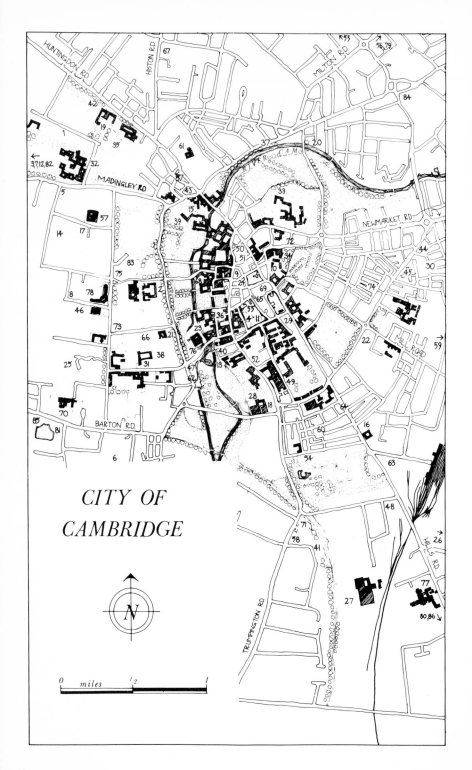

CITY OF
CAMBRIDGE

N

0   miles   ½   1

CAMBRIDGE

In 1953, Sir Nikolaus Pevsner, in the introduction to the Cambridgeshire volume of his *Buildings of England*, castigated the University and the City for preferring timid and old-fashioned architecture. In 1964 he was given the opportunity to revise that view in the Foreword to *Cambridge New Architecture*. The intervening 11 years had changed a lot:

> Since then, all has changed, and we are in the middle of a tremendous activity which no-one can call reactionary, nor indeed conventional. My wishes have been fulfilled to an alarming degree and, in many of the fulfilments, hit back at me. For most of what is going up points in a direction quite different from what I expected or pleaded for. The rational so-called International Modern of the Thirties abortively presented to Cambridge by Walter Gropius in his designs for Christs never gained an entrée. Instead, it is a much more recent irrational International Modern that spreads. The result is a number of buildings with plenty of character, no timidity whatsoever, and a last-minute-up-to-dateness which is certainly a novel element in the history of Cambridge architecture. The best architecture of the International Modern of the Thirties started from an analysis of functions and proceeded to work on how best to provide for them. What is visible in the innovations expresses them, and the rationalism inherent in this procedure expresses itself in a crisp, clear carefully detailed, neutral style. Is this style dead now, as Cambridge seems to indicate? Has it been wholly replaced by a free-for-all, or architecture-for-architecture's sake? Not wholly . . . but by and large the major new buildings want to be masters rather than servants of the actors in them.

In his revised Introduction, the second Edition of *Cambridgeshire* in 1970 Pevsner went further:

> Now architecture tends to be over-dramatic, aggressive, and highly individual, and committees lap it up, even when carried to the excesses of the Faculty of History and the new Zoology and Mathematics Building on the site north of Downing Street. The result of this dare-devil attitude of committees anyway is that Cambridge is now one of the happiest hunting-grounds in Britain for specimens of the architectural style and fashions of the 1960s large and small, elephants as well as butterflies.

It would be difficult to improve on Pevsner's judgement. Cambridge, like Oxford, has become a museum of post-war intellectual architecture, which flourished in the benign climate of *avant-garde* dons, a University-controlled town, and more than the usual quantities of cash to spend on monuments.

Occasionally, the Town managed to cause a hiccup. The 1937 proposal by Walter Gropius and Maxwell Fry for Christ's College (see page 16) was too far ahead of its time: as was Denys Lasdun's Science Complex on the New Museums site, consisting of three high-rise blocks with linked linear blocks. Despite seductive photographs demonstrating how delicately the high-rise towers would appear juxtaposed behind the pinnacles of King's College Chapel, one must be grateful that the sky-line was not breached. Another abortive high-rise scheme was the competition entry by Architects' Co-Partnerhip for Burrells Field. Yet perhaps Cambridge's most significant 'fish that got away' was the proposed shopping centre by Piano & Rogers in the late-Victorian Kite area in south-east inner Cambridge. The plan was (and is) for a regional shopping centre, the execution of which would have demolished a large area of mixed housing and shops of the old-fashioned type.

At the time of going to press, the future of the Kite is still in doubt. However, its survival to date, coupled with the rehabilitation of nearby cottages of the same date, and the increasing amount of small-scale rebuilding work carried out by the City Architects' Department, reflects the mirror image to the grand buildings constructed by the Colleges. There has been some very good small-scale work carried out throughout Cambridge irrespective of the Colleges, and as money for major college building declines, so the importance of the other work increases. The commercial development in the axis between Regent Street and the station should also be noted. In general, it is of mediocre quality, sometimes sinking to the deplorable. Such judgements are, of course, based on the fact that this is Cambridge: the same buildings could well have been welcomed had they been constructed in Bedford or Ipswich.

Although many college buildings have been perpetrated behind high college precinct walls, the humbler parts of Cambridge have suffered. The Newmarket Road dual-carriageway has created a scale of its own entirely inappropriate to Cambridge; whilst nearer the centre of town, King Street has been transformed from an old, unpretentious, shopping street into the rear end of Lasdun's Christ's College on the right, and Smith and Hutton's neo-mediaeval on the left.

Cambridge City between the Wars

Little significant construction took place in Cambridge until the Great War had been over for several years. The first notable buildings falling within the period of this book are those designed by M H Baillie Scott, nos **29, 30, 48, 54 and 56 Storey's Way.** Baillie Scott was an Arts and Crafts architect who had designed buildings in Hampstead Garden Suburb, as well as furniture and jewellery, and whose practice — Baillie Scott & Beresford continued to design small houses and cottages into the 1930s. These houses have the steep pitched roofs, prominent chimney stacks, overhanging (but trimmed) eaves, projected porches and mellow brickwork of the 'olde English' style and particularly fine leaded stair windows. The dining room is the largest apartment. [1]

Mark Potter

The first major development was the **Memorial
Court, Clare College** designed by Sir Giles Gilbert
Scott in 1923-1924, the first college building beyond
the Backs. Two and three storeys of delicate neo-
Georgian buildings constructed of a yellowy-grey brick
enclose a restful T-shaped courtyard. The colonnaded
archway on the east looks back to the old college: on
the west the Memorial Court was closed between
1931-1934 by the new **University Library,** also by Sir
Giles Gilbert Scott. This is a large courtyard building
with a gigantic tower which serves as a stack room. Its
interior is pleasant to use, and the predominantly
'open-stack' layout is popular. Despite the growing
fashion for this period of architecture, the building's
heaviness cannot be avoided. Scott designed the
building soon after being consultant to the exterior of
Battersea Power Station. Contemporary (although
visually illiterate) critics of the building said that he
merely used the drawings for a second time. Their
suspicions appeared to be confirmed when at the
official opening, King George V described the developments as *both a power house and a testing station of
educational activities.*

From 1929 onwards Sir Herbert Baker was employed
to extend **Downing College,** which he did by closing
off that great grassy campus on the west side. Despite
similarities with the original buildings, Baker's look
twentieth century and dull withal. His three storeys
into Wilkins' original two simply would not go.
Pevsner claimed that Baker had been *far too convinced of
himself.* By 1930 the rule of the traditionalists was being
challenged. Between 1927-1929 Raymond McGrath
(later the Decoration Consultant for BBC studios) had
redecorated the interior of the Victorian house **Finella**
in Queens Road, for Mansfield Forbes: a building
which three years later was still said to be 'drawing
large audiences'. The hall was roofed in green glass,
the walls covered in metal leaf, and the floor was
polished black. Glass of different sorts and colours was
used throughout the house. On entering **Finella,** one
was aware of moving into a very special place. In 1931

13

Mark Potter

the **White House, 1 Conduit Head Road** was
designed by George Checkley. (As the '30s progressed
and the modern styles predominated, more and more
buildings were christened 'white house'.) It is very
pure, black and white, and symmetrical. There are two
principal storeys, with two bedrooms opening on to a
roof terrace on the third. It is a simple rectangle and
the first-floor bedrooms undoubtedly suffer from the
way their windows are curtailed to fit the external
ziggurat fenestration. It is now rather obscured by the
block of flats to the front.

In the same year Sir Edwin Lutyens began **Benson
Court** for Magdalen College. Only the west wing of a
much larger development was completed: thin red
bricks with a sprinkling of purple, the whole being a
combination of Tudor gables, massive chimney stacks
and neo-Baroque stone doorways. Great fun has been
had with the five different staircase baluster details —
evidently for the guidance of drunk students.

In 1931, H C Hughes began the **Royal Society
Mond Laboratory** beside the Cavendish Labs, off
Corn Exchange Street. Specially designed to
accommodate high-intensity magnetic equipment and
very low-temperature tests, the scheme is rectangular,
designed around a central hall. Its glory is the entrance
hall and staircase: a pure 1930s curved tower, the
punctured walls being rendered in cream. The brick
exterior is less pure, but enlivened by an engagingly
fierce crocodile carved by Eric Gill, who described it as
the dragon of science devouring Culture.

In 1932 Marshall Sisson completed **31 Madingley
Road,** a rather grander house than the White House
but with similarities: again two storey with a roof
garden, like a covered shelter in place of the bedrooms.
There the similarity ends. This building is in brick,
with neo-Dutch banding above the windows which
themselves do not have the same clarity as the other

4 Mond Laboratory

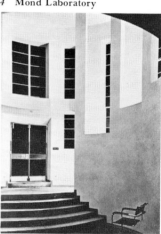

(H C Hughes)

5 31 Madingley Road

(RIBA Library)

6 26 Millington Road   RIBA Library

7 Salix, Conduit Head Road

8 2 Sylvester Road

house. The garage is attached at one side to balance the pergola at the other. The house might be compared to Sisson's other house — **26 Millington Road (1934)** which is rendered, with neater windows — the banding above them removed, and the third storey formalised above the stair tower.

In 1932, Checkley's second building — **Thurso, 2 Conduit Head Road,** showed some advance over the White House. Once more two storeys with terrace on the roof, Thurso has a double-height hall with a splendid semi-circular feature being made of the staircase. The purist box approach of the White House has given way to an asymmetrical building one whose rooms being above the hall, is at a half level higher than the others and has a projecting balcony. The main entrance front has none of the interest of the garden front. Although concrete frame and brick infill, the building is rendered in cream to give the stylistic appearance of being mass concrete, required by the International Style.

The following year H C Hughes, shedding his former housing habits (as in 94 Barton Road and 31 Storey's Way) produced **Salix, Conduit Head Road,** whose low ground storey, L-shaped in plan, is surmounted by much smaller L-shaped upper storey overlooking a roof terrace, like the bridge of a square stranded ocean liner. The first building in Cambridge to make a specific point of windows turning the corners: it demonstrated the independence of the walls from the structure. The house of Professor Postan, **2 Sylvester Road.** is much plainer by comparison: the British version of modern-squat two-storey brick block, shallow projecting bay in the living room. Windows are simple unadorned strip windows. The house is now part of the development plan for Robinson College.

In 1934, the first of three major developments by J Murray Easton, of Stanley Hall, Easton and Robertson was completed. That was the **Zoological Libraries, Corn Exchange Street,** an L-shaped development with a tail sticking out of the L. The style is probably becoming fashionable, and was certainly functional: a five-storey brick-banded building with almost continuous windows. Its saving grace is the mild curve which it presents to the street. It was followed, in 1937, by the **Market Hill Buildings** for Gonville and Caius, a reasonably elegant, modern building facing Market Hill of four storeys above a colonnade: typically '30s in fenestration metal windows and the banding, but not as visually arresting as it would have been in white render rather than stone. From St Mary's Court, the development is more traditional — not metal, nor horizontal, windows, but vertical Georgian sashes. The rooms inside must have been some of the most up to date in Cambridge of the time. Pevsner considered this to be the best modern inter-war building in Cambridge.

9 **Market Hill building**

(Mark Potter)

10 **Walter Gropius' proposal for Christ's College** (by permission of the Master and Fellows of Christ's College)

More or less contemporary, and totally different, was the proposal in 1936-37 by Walter Gropius and Maxwell Fry for a new Court for **Christ's College** in Hobson Street. Pevsner's view was that *the best architecture of the International Modern of the Thirties started from an analysis of functions and proceeded to work on how best to provide for them. What is visible in the innovations expresses them, and the rationalism inherent in this procedure expresses itself in a crisp, clear, carefully detailed, neutral style.* That is wishful thinking. The Gropius/Fry scheme has the stylistic spoor of its epoch — a curved, glass-enclosed staircase, curved corners over-sailing roofs, a penthouse, and even a drive in the forecourt: none of the compromises of the Easton scheme.

That year, Charles Holden, of Adams, Holden, Pearson (London Transport and London University) completed the **Cavendish High Tension Laboratory,** off Corn Market Street. Very plain: the requirements were really for a giant shed for high-tension experimental work. There are minor rooms at either end with an internal gallery running along one wall. Externally it is really a giant screen wall of banded brickwork and few openings.

11 School of Anatomy

Mark Potter

12 Shawms

Mark Potter

13 Fen Court, Peterhouse

Hughes & Bicknell

In 1938, Murray Easton produced what, in parts, is his most distinctive Cambridge building, the **School of Anatomy**, an L-shaped building in brick, in advance of its time. The staircase is in glass block and the marginally overhanging flat roof and rectangular clere storey lights beneath is attractive. The lift tower is subtly curved.

In the same year, Justin Blanco White, a Don's wife, produced the last major Modern house in Cambridge before the War, **Shawms** in Conduit Head Road. Unlike all the others, it is timber framed and horizontally boarded. Its garden facade is almost ageless and dateless. Writing to Jeremy Gould, the architect declared her intentions: *What we aimed at doing was: a sunny house, full of light, the whole floor area light and warm enough to use, i.e. no shadowy corners; also all the rooms seeming spacious by opening to the very beautiful garden, and having pure shapes.*

In 1939, S E Urwin, the County Architect, completed the **County Clinic,** on Castle Hill, a small, single-storey building arranged round the central waiting hall. It has touches of Art Deco: banded brick, a jagged entrance, and strip windows.

Back down in the Centre, larger arrivals were being finished off, the most obvious being **The Guild Hall,** Market Hill, by C Cowles-Voysey, 1939, a grand neo-Georgian design, by Voysey's son. It is a much larger building than it seems from Market Hill and is relatively unfriendly. Because of its location it had to dispense with the panache of the same architect's contemporary Town Hall in Watford.

13

Hughes & Bicknell

Meanwhile, down little St Mary's Lane, past St Mary the Less, and behind the fine brick wall screening the Royal Garden Hotel, Hughes and Bicknell had managed to inflict a *modern* college building on Cambridge whilst nobody noticed. **Fen Court, Peterhouse,** was one of three designs offered to the college, the other two being traditional. It is L-shaped, with a Scandinavian glass cupola on the heel, sombre, banded brown brick, one wing on piloti, and the overall effect Dutch. The later additions on the roof detract considerably from the scheme's character.

CAMBRIDGE POST WAR

14

11 Wilberforce Road. David Robert's own house — one of his earliest buildings in Cambridge — dates from the post-war materials shortage and rationing of timber and steel. Completed in 1952 as a single-storey, L-shaped building, it was extended to two storeys in 1957. To some extent influenced by the house designed by Mrs Cosens in 1936 at No. 9 Wilberforce Road, this house is similar to contemporary schemes by Roberts for Magdalene College. It has a simple plan, austerity detailing, and colour washed brick.

Benson and Mallory Courts Magdalene College   *15*
David Roberts (Christophe Grillet, Geoffrey Clark, Gerald Craig, Keith Garbett)
1952-70
The result of an 18-year scheme to increase the accommodation in Magdalene College without destroying its innate historic character unlike the Lutyens 1931 proposal. Some of the older infill houses look their age (just post-Festival of Britain) but little could improve the four-storey block by the river save a pitched roof. The new dark red brick building provides a firm boundary to Magdalene property, and has car parking beneath undergraduates' rooms. It is the most heavily 'architectural' development of the site.

Snoek

Highsett Hills Road 16
Eric Lyons and Partners
1958-65 Wates Ltd and Rattee & Kett Ltd

The only large work in East Anglia by the late Eric Lyons, Highsett consists of flats and houses on a site originally designated for a high-rise tower of bachelor flats. The building facing Hills Road is a quadrangle of flats raised on piloti so as to give views into the interior of the courtyard. Materials — for example tile hanging — are not very East Anglian. The courtyard of flats has a neat, slightly Scandinavian feel about it and is the best part of the schemes. Highsett would not have been particularly special were it not for the fact that other British flat developments have been so appalling. The modern terraced houses behind were an exciting novelty at the time.

Colin Westwood

3 Clarkson Road 17
Trevor Dannatt
1958 Brudenell Builders

The rural image intellectualised in Cambridge. This house, chunky from the exterior, belies the openness of its interior. Advantage has been taken of sloping ground to provide a ground floor with one half lower than the other: thus the staircase rises out of the dining room to the living room. The strip window in the living room being taken round the corner is a '30s regurgitation. Interior is interesting; exterior pretty Teutonic. One is reminded of C F A Voysey's criticism of modern architecture as *square box, roofless buildings*.

Extension, Faculty of Architecture Building *18*
Scroope Terrace
Colin St John Wilson (with Alex Hardy)
1959 Coulson & Son Ltd
Highly influential, crisp two-storey brick and concrete
extension with single-storey brick paved link to early
Victorian Scroope Terrace. Very much a period piece,
with banding of concrete and brick, sideways pivot
doors, and cleverly placed windows.

Fitzwilliam College Huntingdon Road *19*
Denys Lasdun and Partners
1959 Johnson and Bailey
A most peculiar development: the plan provides for
the completion of the main buildings for the college —
library, hall, service rooms etc, with the facility for
residential accommodation to be extended in a courtyard around that core when money becomes available.
The building is a mixture of styles: the residential
blocks are flat roofed and look topless; the parlour has
a jagged pointed pitched roof; the library is rather
heavily lead faced with projecting windows, and poking
up behind is the glass enclosed concrete hall roof.

20

Leigh

**Corpus Christi and Sidney Sussex
Boat House** Victoria Avenue
David Roberts (Christophe Grillett)
1959
A delightful, neat two-storey building with symmetrical spiral staircases at either end. Storage for
boats below (solid) club rooms and
changing rooms above (light).

Donat

22
Parkside Swimming Pool
East Road, Cambridge
City Surveyor's Department
(R J Wyatt)
1960
A simple box, with a glazed gable and walls, ingeniously planned. With hindsight it can be seen to lack the razzamatazz of modern swimming pools in terms of shape, colour and configurations.

23
Erasmus Building Queens' College
Sir Basil Spence & Partners
1960
Four-storey building closing off Friar's Court. Brick, rather arbitrary pattern of windows on the exterior, and flat-roofed terrace with concrete pergola. Interior furnishings also designed by the architects.

Harvey Court Gonville & Caius, West Road **21**
Sir Leslie Martin and Colin St John Wilson
(Patrick Hodgkinson)
1962 William Sindall Ltd
An extremely formally planned hostel for 100 undergraduates and some Fellows in suburban Cambridge. The architects have re-interpreted the quadrangle: the building is designed around a square, three sides of which face into the centre. The fourth side, isolated from the remainder by two flights of stairs faces out into the garden. The central court is a storey above ground level (hence the stairs) and contains a number of service rooms, the breakfast room and the common room (their roofs confusing the courtyard above). Each floor of students' rooms is stepped back from the previous one, so that the roof of the lower storey forms the outside terrace for the rooms above. There is something very elegant about wide flights of steps, spacious — if echoing — ambulatories within each block, and the gradual recession of the elegantly detailed brick buildings as they get higher. There are affinities here with Lasdun's developments, but completely lacking Lasdun's preoccupation with making every unit show. These buildings have influenced many subsequent developments — most notably John Winter's new housing at Milton Keynes. It is a self-contained, rather cloistral, development, maintaining an extremely hard edge between the hostel and the garden beyond. One wonders whether those students with rooms gazing over communal balconies into other rooms, and facing into the hard central courtyard, feel as privileged as those who face out into the trees.

ACP

King's College Hostel Market Hill   *24*
Architects Co-Partnership (Kenneth Capon, Alan Comrie-Smith)
1962
Controversial building on a prominent site whose white bricks were originally loathed. Hard now to see what the fuss was about: the building is neither one thing nor the other and seems foreshortened by the way the top storey steps back to provide a balcony. The string-courses in slate make the building look heavy.

Arup

George Thompson Building   *25*
Leckhampton House Grange Road
Arup Associates
1964 William Sindall Ltd
This building provides a community for Fellows, 24 research students and graduates in the superb eight-acre garden of an Edwardian house. Accommodation is provided in two blocks, and (as in Boulton House) the appearance is governed by the white H-frame structure. Typical of Arup buildings, these blocks fit snugly into the garden and are delicately detailed as the exterior and provide a covered — almost cloistral — walk at ground level. See also St John's College, Oxford. The only jarring note is the side brick panels.

26

Leigh

St Bede's Secondary School Birdwood Road
David Roberts
1961-62
Pevsner considered this school *Without any doubt the best post-war school in Cambridge.* A very neat, two-storey, red brick and glass, attractively symmetrical building, this school shows how the formality sought after at Hunstanton could be humanised.

27
Cambridge University Press
Brooklands Avenue
Beard Bennett
Wilkins & Partners
1963
Fairly ordinary offices recently extended. Notable for the printing block which is divided into seven bays and spanned by a steel-ribbed roof curved in two directions.

22

Brecht-Einzig

29

Brecht-Einzig

Masters Lodge, Emmanuel College
Tom Hancock (John S L Edwards)
1964 Kerridge
The Master desired a plain house to replace what Pevsner called an *uncommonly ugly brick villa.* A very formal design in concrete and buttressed brick, on a podium, with a grand double height drawing room study at one end. The private side of the house is in a three-storey block on the north side. An extremely neat if hard and uncompromising building.

30
Cherry Trees Club St Matthews Street
David Roberts (David Davies and John Sargent)
1964
Simple club, flat roof, largely blank from the street ensuring privacy for those inside. Neatly detailed.

William Stone Building Trumpington Street   *28*
Sir Leslie Martin and Colin St John Wilson
1964 Kerridge (Cambridge) Ltd
The first residential college building in Cambridge with a lift since the architects determined to maximise the development vertically so as to take up as little as possible of Peterhouse's former Deer Park. The result is a block of rooms for eight Fellows and 24 students, in splendid grounds. The rooms are spacious, and are arranged in jagged formation facing the garden, with the service rooms at the back on the other side of a wide lobby. The rear presents an elegant, if austere pattern of brick and long strip windows.

Arts Faculty Buildings off Sidgwick Avenue   *31*
Casson Condor & Partners
Stages 1-4 1964 Johnson & Bailey and Kerridge
Part of a comprehensive plan for the Arts Faculty on a site west of the Backs, originally proposed in a competition won in 1952 by Sir Hugh Casson. The main feature is a courtyard created between the Economics and Politics Building, and those of English, Moral Sciences and Languages. The buildings are raised on piloti, encouraging space and cold weather to pass throughout. The architecture is humane but peculiarly lacking architectural bite when compared to some of Cambridge's other gleaming monuments. Post-Festival of Britain picturesqueness.

Churchill College Storeys Way   *32*   Brecht-Einzig
Sheppard Robson
1965 Rattee & Kett Ltd
Brick and concrete quadrangle-based college with
prominent Hall and Chapel. Founded as a memorial
for Sir Winston Churchill, and specialising in Science
and Technology, the College was the outcome of an
architectural competition. Its popular success might be
judged by its RIBA Award in 1968. It is a most
English building; save for the Hall roof, it is languid,
plain, well mannered and well dressed in the fashionable brick and concrete banding of the time. Some
Corbusian echoes (Maison Jaoul) here and there.

North Court, Jesus College *33*
David Roberts (Geoffrey Clark and Philip Durne)
1965 Rattee & Kett Ltd
Seventy bedsits to the north of the old College buildings.
Interesting diagonal planning, allowing each living room to
have its own balcony. The result is restless but not intrusive.

Brecht-Einzig

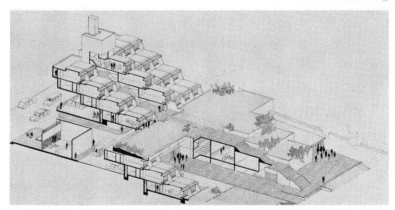

New Court, Christ's College *34*
Denys Lasdun and Partners
1966 John Mowlem and Co Ltd
Another celebrated building, comprising principally
study bedrooms, Fellows' flats, a large hall and recreational facilities. It has been designed primarily with an
inward eye facing its newly created courtyard. The
architect quotes *hills and valleys* as architectural inspiration seeking latent classical qualities such as proportion,
rhythm and repose. There is a clear derivation from
the ziggurats of the East Anglian campus. From the
courtyard side, the development is visually successful,
if slightly overburdened. From the street the development indicates the fundamental penalties of single-
aspect design.

37

New Hall Huntingdon Road 35
Chamberlin Powell & Bon (John Honer)
1966 W & C French, and Johnson & Bailey
A completely new College on a tight site off the
Huntingdon Road originally scheduled to be part of a
new campus with Churchill. Post-Modern before the
term was invented, the Library is barrel vaulted, and
the dining room domed. The latter can be compared to
both a Byzantine Basilica and a concrete spaceship.
Touches of Golden Lane (their earlier prize-winning
scheme in London) in the facades of the sets of rooms.
Fountain Court suffers from minuteness adjacent to the
gigantic bulbous dining room.

New Spring Toilets Chesterton
Road
City Architect's Department
(Colin Derry)
1966
Slightly Festival of Britainish
building, brick walls and over
sailing — visually detached — flat
roof supported on black steel
members.

Kings Lane Development Trumpington Street 36
James Cubitt Fello Atkinson & Partners (John Baker)
1967 Bovis
A unique collaboration between two colleges — King's
and St Catharine's — to develop contiguous land. The
project, much praised by Pevsner, includes residential
accommodation, additional communal rooms for both
colleges and the renovation of King's College Hall.
The added feature of pre-fabricated bathrooms
attached to each room was provided for holiday
conference use. The details particularly the triangulated windows — are pretty weak.

Brecht-Einzig

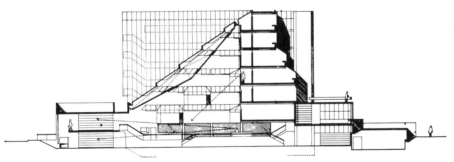

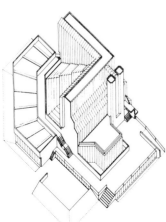

History Faculty Library Sidgwick Avenue   *38*
James Stirling (Michael Wilford)
1967 William Sindall Ltd

Pevsner called it *rude, anti-architecture and actively ugly*. Others hail it as a masterpiece. Ironically it is highly likely that Stirling, given the same commission today, would not take this approach. It is an L-shaped building of harsh red engineering brick, between whose wings there is a veritable cascade of glass which covers the main library area.

Several floors of ancillary accommodation rise above overlooking this space. The building is glittering, and its engineering aesthetic has been extraordinarily influential. The style has been subsequently adapted for buildings ranging in type from houses to fire stations.

Office Building for Longman's Green - Harlow

The Robinson Pool - Bedford

The Senate House - University of East Anglia

King's Lynn District General Hospital

Just four of the many contracts carried out in the Eastern Region by

Sindall

William Sindall p.l.c.
Sindall Construction Ltd
Sindall Concrete Products Ltd
Sindall (Norwich) Ltd

Cambridge London & Norwich

Cripps Building, St John's College *39*
Powell & Moya (B Knight)
1967 John Laing
One of the most important new buildings in Cambridge, on a site between the River Cam and the Bin Brook. It contains 200 new sets of rooms, principally for undergraduates, but including eight larger sets for Fellows. As such it is one of the largest new developments in Cambridge, and certainly the most significant modern addition to the Backs. Effectively a zig-zagged four-storey block, the building creates the impression of enclosing space in traditional courtyard fashion. Built of the most splendid materials — the clients wanted a building that would last — the principal impact is derived from its startling whiteness and contrast between horizontal and vertical. There is a penthouse on the top.

De Mare

41

Snoek

Dryden House Newton Road
Eric Lyons Cunningham Partnership
1968
A very nice scheme of 9 two-bedroom flats for Trinity College graduates.

University Centre Granta Place *40*
Howell Killick Partridge & Amis (Roy Murphy)
1967 William Sindall Ltd
Colloquially known as the Grad Pad, the building salivates over every joint. Superb materials — stone, pre-cast concrete panels, lead covered stairs, oak and other timbers — see particularly the grand Dining Hall. Splendid views from within. The building operates in the tradition of a nineteenth-century club.

Arup

Boulton House Wychfield Estate, Huntingdon Rd *42*
Arup Associates
1968 William Sindall Ltd
One of the many developments to be seen along the
Huntingdon Road, Boulton House provides 32 study-
bedrooms and two sets for Fellows on three upper
floors, with common rooms on the ground floor. The
proportion of the scheme is governed by the study-
bedrooms unit, whose smallness is relieved by the
projecting bay windows, and generous window seat —
which gives the room something of the scale of the
grounds outside. This is a typical Arup development in
the clarity of its appearance and structure.

Brecht-Einzig

Kettles Yard Gallery Northampton Street *43*
Sir Leslie Martin and David Owers
1970 Kidman & Sons Ltd
From the outside it would be hard to spot what was
new in the group surrounding St Peter's Church. The
Gallery is really an extension to the house of Mr Jim
Ede wherein he displays his own collection. A further
part of the development is a self-contained but
connected gallery with its own entrance, which is used
for temporary exhibitions. The Gallery is entered from
the house itself, and across a bridge at first-floor level
from which it opens out into upper and lower levels.
These are visually interconnected, and form a series of
roof-lit descending spaces.

44
The Howard Mallet Club
St Matthews Street
City Architect's Department
(G Logie)
1968 Builder: Grant & Dodson Ltd
A very sleek image for a civic building: single storey, designed like a
glazed pavilion on a slightly raised
grass plinth. Neatly detailed glass
curtain wall capped by a simple
black fascia.

45
East Road
David Roberts and Geoffrey Clark
(David Davies and Philip Durne)
1959-68
Comprehensive redevelopment including terraced houses, flats, old
people's home and parking. One of
Cambridge's few essays into the
large-scale redevelopment that
afflicted most of Britain at the time.
It preserved a certain humanity of
scale and detail absent in the similar
large scale redevelopments elsewhere. No high rise: all brick.

Architectural Review

Clare Hall Herschel Road   *46*
Ralph Erskine's Architekt Kontor with
Twist & Whitley (B Ahlquist, M Linnett)
1969 F B Thackray & Co Ltd
A post-graduate college, founded by Clare College,
providing common rooms, dining room, seminar
rooms and houses catering for both single and married
post-graduates. Nothing in such a bare description
leads one to expect the excitement of this building.
Situated in an old garden the design is the only
building in Cambridge by Ralph Erskine, in association
with the local architects Twist & Whitley. A number of
points lead one forward to Erskine's subsequently
much more famous development at Byker in Newcastle.
First, the concept of openness, whereby the public is
encouraged to pass through what would otherwise be a
cloistered college atmosphere between one street and
the next. Second, the use of bright colour — particularly the two-tone, red-stained timberwork; third, the
delight in details evinced spectacularly by the method
of collecting rainwater and turning it into a feature.

Darwin College Silver Street   *47*
Howell, Killick & Partridge, Amis (R Murphy)
1970 Kerridge (Cambridge) Ltd
Darwin was the first graduate college to be founded in
Cambridge in modern times, founded in 1964 by
Gonville and Caius, St John's and Trinity. It is a
composition of three fine ancient houses on the west
side of Silver Street, with two completely new additions
— the one a residential block with 34 bed-sitting rooms
on three floors and attic, the other an octagonal dining
hall, set on first-floor level, around the corner. The
buildings are straightforward HKPA brutalist: natural
pine on the interior, the dining hall capped by a top-lit
pyramid. The brick, vertically modelled exteriors are
wholly unsuccessful. The college involved the rehabilitation and conversion of the older houses, in one case
back to the restitution of what is believed to be its
original Victorian character — including William
Morris wallpaper and leather-covered Victorian
furniture.
    Note also: **New east building** by **David Roberts**
(1981).

48
Great Ouse House
Clarendon Road
Edward D Mills & Partners
(G Partridge)
1970 Johnson & Bailey
Headquarters Building for the Great
Ouse River Authority in rather
undistinguished   suburban
Cambridge. Neat,   five-storey
building with recessed ground
storey.

Darwin College Dining Hall

HKPA

Brecht-Einzig

Downing College   *49*
Howell Killick Partridge & Amis (Prof. W G Howell,
R J Murphy)
1970 Coulson & Son Ltd
There is more to this scheme than meets the eye: in
addition to the new Combination Room (the most
famous part of the development) there are new
kitchens, a college office block, and a re-organisation of
the original William Wilkins buildings dating from
1818. No self-respecting college wants a kitchen facing
its Fellows' garden, and it is therefore screened behind
a high wall, against which the new Combination Room
is set as a pavilion in the garden. The grand-neo-
classical pediment of Wilkins is echoed in a mini,
scaled down version by the broken pediments of the
new Combination Room. The fact that the new room
is on the same plinth as the main hall makes it seem
like a toy mimic of the original. Inside it is a *jeu
d'esprit:* a clear post and beam concrete structure, with
the roof pattern following that clearly indicated on the
exterior.

Bruno de Hamel

51

Heffers Bookshop Trinity Street
Austin-Smith, Lord
(Peter J Lord)
1970 Wiltshiers
Part of a larger development for
Trinity College, the shop uses four
levels most below ground. Very
clean lines, superb central volume,
although the fascia is rather heavy
for the buildings under which it is
situated.

Wolfson Building, Trinity College   *50*
Architects Co-Partnership (Michael Powers)
1972 William Sindall Ltd
A back-yard development of 90 undergraduate rooms
carefully detailed in expensive materials. Distinctive for
its ziggurat shape and ungainly, projecting, fin-like
roof lights. Typical banding of concrete and brick of
the period. The building shows a positive, stamen-like
determination not to adopt the traditional Cambridge
courtyard form.

52
Cosin Court Trumpington Street
David Roberts and Geoffrey Clark
(Gerald Craig, Michael Driver)
1970 Coulson & Sons Ltd
Interesting enclosed housing
development for Peterhouse. Pitched
roof perched on top of tall brick
columns rising through three-and-a-
half storeys.

Kings Hedges Estate

City Surveyor's Department, followed by
City Architect's Department
1955 onwards
Earlier stages known locally as the 'Berlin Wall': later stages (not yet christened) include gestures towards a hazy memory of ye olde Englande. Back to red pantiles, to corbels, and to heavily detailed and patterned brickwork.

St Mary's Convent School Bateman Street   *54*
David Roberts (Christophe Grillet, Peter Hall, Tim Matthias)
1973
A large development only part of which is obvious from the street, and best viewed from Panton Street. Brick banded with glazing, with vertically glazed stair towers.

57

Brecht-Einzig

New Museums Corn Exchange Street   *55*
Arup Associates
1971 Trollope & Colls/William Sindall Ltd
This building is the disproportionate rump of a larger unfinished development. Pevsner thought it *Piranesian*. Typical Arup clarity of structure — (architects who like to see through their buildings instead of looking at them) but very heavy lead covered stair towers and top fascias. More beautiful in plan and structure than in fact. Includes the Department of Physics, Zoology, Chemical Engineering and Metallurgy.

Wolfson Court Clarkson Road
David Roberts & Geoffrey Clark
(Gerald Craig and Brendan Woods)
1971 Coulson & Son Ltd
Residential buildings and communal facilities for students at Girton College. A touch of St Tropez in the bright orange pantiles, and slatted shutters. The timberwork — particularly in the communal rooms — seems to have run riot.

56 (right)
Power House Sewage Works, Milton Road
City Architect's Department
(T Jordan)
1971 Kier Ltd
RIBA Eastern Region Certificate of Merit (1973). A heavily Stirling-influenced box on a bright red brick plinth, with billowing space-frame above. Surprisingly crisp for a Sewage Works.

56

C

Brecht-Einzig

Evelyn Nursing Home Trumpington Road   *58*
Cambridge Design (D Thurlow, R Davies,
S Furness, D Thompson)
1974 Coulson & Son Ltd
Nursing accommodation in a simple L-shaped block.
The design is so neat and yet beautiful that the scheme
won the RIBA Award in 1976. The main staircase,
which is entirely glazed, is at the heel of the L, with
two wings radiating from it. On the garden side the
nurses' rooms are contained in what is effectively the
roof, linked by a top-lit corridor. The lavatories
and kitchens face out onto the entrance courtyard.
From the back, the scheme presents simply a huge,
dark sloping roof punctuated by the inset windows and
balconies of the nurses' bedrooms, and the great glazed
staircase. The entrance courtyard, by contrast, has the
character of a black-and-white brick farmhouse.

59
D & H Contractors Ltd
Hooper Street
C J Bourne (C H Brook)
1970 Kidman & Sons Ltd
A simple block overlooking the
railway: neat design, upper two
storeys oversailing ground storey,
contrast dark wood timber frames
with concrete panels, and bright
orange curved fire escape staircase
on the gable.

City of Cambridge

Newtown 2a Coronation Street   *60*
City Architect's Department (P Frost)
1974 M Wynn Ltd
Local authority houses and flats in an East Anglian
neo-vernacular matching the existing grain and scale of
Cambridge. The details are very thoroughly thought
through. The end by the Panton Arms is distinctly
more effective than the interior of the scheme. Perhaps
a trifle forced, and the scale of spaces too wide. Yet
worth a detour.

61
Shire Hall Extension Castle Hill
County Architects' Department
(John Pook)
1974
Known as the Octagon, this extension at the rear of the neo-Georgian
County Hall (H H Dunn, 1931)
had to create its own identity and
almost succeeds, with three large
landscaped floors of offices clad in
honey-coloured concrete.

Brecht-Einzig

Granta Inn Newnham   *62*
Lyster Grillet Harding (P Sparks)
1976 P Cope & Co
Lyster Grillet and Harding have been involved in a number of pub conversions and extensions, including the Granta Inn and the Pike and Eel. Of the two, the Granta is more interesting, being a Bar cantilevered out over the mill pond with a pair of symmetrical stairs from each gable leading down to a landing-stage. A veritable punt trap. The architects were also responsible for *Scurfield's* shop front in King Street notable perhaps for its Saxon round-headed doorways: a shop front that creates its own style in flat contradiction of the existing character of the houses in which it is set.

Jupiter House

Dawson Strange

Hills Road and Station Road Development   *63*
Nos. 72-80 Hills Road, 82-88 Hills Road, Jupiter House, Station Road
Fitzroy Robinson & Partners (P A Golden, J R Saunders, J R Johnson, L F Barber, R Casanovas, A R Goodden)
Three Crowns House, 72-80, is one of the better developments along Hills Road, and the fussy 82-88 the worst. Along Station Road, Jupiter House is one of three blocks whose architectural effect is achieved by the concrete frames standing proud of the glazing behind. The proportions and the way in which the building sits on a brick plinth are quite pleasing. Great Eastern House (1957) by H M Powell is inoffensive for a large building. But even good office buildings show a depressing lack of peculiarly local character.

64
Regent Street Developments
Nos. 49-53, 94, 95-97, 93
Fitzroy Robinson & Partners
(P A Golden, R Bunten, L F Barber, R Casanovas, N R Ruffles, A R Goodden)
Four significant developments in the one area of Cambridge, completed in four years by the same architectural team. In most cases opportunities are missed. but numbers 49-53 and number 94 are good of their type.

35

Fisher House Guildhall Place (right)   *65*
Gerard Goalen and Partner (M Goalen Goalen)
1976 Rattee & Kett
A difficult project which included the rehabilitation of several older buildings, and the construction of a new, clerestorey lit Assembly Room at one end. The building is chamferred at the corners, and its clerestorey projects slightly over the wall. From the inside, the brickwork is of some interest. The development includes some undergraduate living accommodation, a weekday Chapel and a library.

Fisher House   Snoek

Faculty of Music West Road   *66*
Sir Leslie Martin with Colen Lumley and Ivor Richards
1977 (Phase 1) Coulson & Son Ltd, William Sindall Ltd
A Music Hall for 500 people, with lecture and seminar rooms, practice rooms etc. to follow. A popular hall, but rather primitive in appearance. No concessions to the current trends for decoration and heightened use of colour. Because it is a phased development no coherent judgement can yet be made of its external appearance.

Symons House

Symons House 132-160 Histon Road (right)   *67*
Darbourne & Darke (J Rawlings, M Johnson)
1977 Kerridge (Cambridge) Ltd
Dreary suburban Cambridge provides the only example of Darbourne and Darke's work in the area. Some typical features: the dark brick, projecting bay windows, the vertically proportioned casement windows, and contrast between planes. Well worth a second look despite the overbearing if popular asbestos tiles.

Charles

Trinity Hall
Mackley

Trinity Hall (left) *68*
David Roberts & Geoffrey Clark (Martin Goalen, John Ellis, Michael James)
1975 Coulson & Son Ltd

A high quality example of what is now becoming frequent in Cambridge in the absence of available green field sites: the translation of backland areas, and inconvenient rooms into new purpose-designed buildings. This job included re-planning existing rooms, as well as creating a new Junior Combination Room, Lecture/Television Room, Music and Seminar Rooms. A new high level courtyard reached by a flight of steps has been formed and the use of timber and mellow tiles is particularly effective.

Lion Yard Redevelopment and City Library *69*
PettyCury
Arup Associates with Fewster & Partners
1975 Bovis Construction Ltd

Cambridge's only concession to the modern obsession with shopping centres — (although it has tried hard enough in the Kite) — the Lion Yard Redevelopment occupies a site ranging from the corner of Market Square through to Sidney Street. As a shopping centre, it is relatively undistinguished, arranged around a T-shaped pedestrian mall. With the possible exception of Culpeppers, the shops are the standard one would find from Truro to Sunderland, in an envelope which is by no means one of the finest in modern Britain. From the street, the facade is one of brown brick contrasted with a white concrete structure from which various shop signs project. What makes this scheme particular is the Library above the central mall at first-floor level, which includes an outdoor sitting area and contains a genuinely different atmosphere to the shopping mall below.

70

Leigh

Wolfson College Barton Road
Ferrey & Mennim
(C F G Liversedge)
1977

A new graduate college in western suburban Cambridge arranged around two courtyards with the main college buildings at the centre. Despite excellent materials, and a peaceful layout, the building design itself is fairly characterless: the buttresses are feeble, the projecting bays are shallow, and the college as a whole would be immeasurably improved by an oversailing roof.

Charles

Queensway Housing Trumpington Road *71*
Cambridge Design (D Thurlow, S Furness,
C Cowper, Di Haig, R Lyon)
1978 Johnson & Bailey Ltd
A bulls-eye in a gable at the traffic lights in Trumpington Road, indicates the presence of this development of two blocks of 79 flats for the Granta Housing Society. There are seven different flat types in the three-storey buildings, each flat within having a dual aspect. Essentially rather sombre brick boxes with a simple pitched roof, this project is rendered quite extraordinary by the inventive way with which balconies and access stairs have been tacked on. There are clear influences from Ralph Erskine at Byker and Newmarket, particularly in the use of clear plastic roofing for the balconies and staircases.

73
St Chad's Development
St Catharine's College,
Grange Road
James Cubitt Fello Atkinson & Partners (John Baker and Peter Gray)
1978
Odd development of octagonal study bedrooms snaking around an existing house.

74

Donat

Manor Place King Street *72*
Ivor Smith & Cailey Hutton (Håkan Frick, Alan Drury)
1978 Johnson & Bailey Ltd
Worth looking at. An attempt to recreate an historic street front in two long, parallel blocks of flats. Despite ingenious neo-mediaeval timber-framed windows at first-floor level, the street scenery fails in intent probably because it is too weak: the road has been allowed to be widened, and the detail on the new buildings is not sufficiently strong to create the impression the architects were seeking.

Donat

18 and 20 John Street
Keith Garbett
1978 John Brignell
Development of flats for single women over 40, with vague stylistic references to post-modernism in the exterior. Popular with residents.

Adrian and Butler Houses   Austin

Adrian House and Butler House Grange Road   75
David Roberts & Geoffrey Clark (Barry Brown)
1978
Distinct signs of Roberts and Clark branching out with
something more vivid than usual. Two blocks of flats
for Trinity College graduates, with projecting bay
windows, virtually continuous strip glazing beneath the
eaves and clay pantiles. Italianate.

77

Homerton College Hills Road
Lyster Grillet & Harding
(Christophe Grillet, Peter Sparks)
1964-78
Fourteen-year period of development, culminating recently in the
Biology Building. This latter, more
traditional than its predecessors, has
a rather neat, square chimney.
Careful investigators may also find a
nursery by Maxwell Fry, 1940.

Cripps Court Queens' College   76
Powell, Moya & Partners (E Lloyd, R Burr)
1979 John Laing Ltd
Across the Mathematical Bridge from the older college.
This scheme contains 146 sets of rooms, arranged on
three sides of a courtyard, the fourth side containing
the new dining hall. The rooms are stacked in the
traditional staircase pattern, and the three wings of
accommodation have some affinities with the St John's
Building: the contrast between the horizontal and the
vertical, and the brightness of the structure contrasting
with the dark glass between. The building however
lacks the St John's lightness: the columns which rise
through four storeys just disappear: They do not
terminate. The roof of the dining hall — although
splendid internally — has a heavy appearance. The
Powell and Moya clarity is still there, but the lightness
of touch has gone.

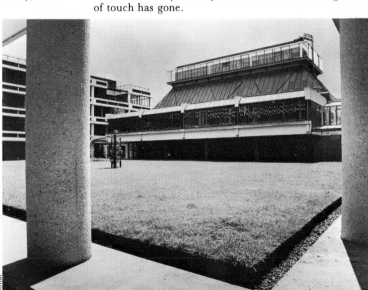

Donat

Architects' Journal

Robinson College Grange Road *78*
Gillespie Kidd & Coia (YRM Executive Architects)
1981
An outstanding building, in parts one of the best
European post-war pieces of architecture. Designed to
enclose one end of the site, the college is in two parallel
L-shaped blocks. The street frontage contains the
Chapel, the administration and the Library: the glories
of the College. The inner layer contains terraces of
student rooms. The latter are interesting but not
exceptional and have some operational curiosities.
The fact that their access is a storey higher than the
principal central 'street' adds to their remoteness and
hardness. But the Chapel, with its bronze decorations
and outstanding brickwork; and the timber felicities in
the Library makes one wonder that the concept was
created under competition conditions. The squared
trellis and ziggurat fenestration have created their own
rapidly developing style in the United Kingdom.

79
Napp Laboratories
Cambridge Science Park,
North Road
Arthur Erickson
Unfinished
Major scientific laboratories
enclosed in a three-storied moated
shed. The walls are canted, the
gables glazed and the overall
impression comparatively heavy if
elegant. Yet it is good to see a
Canadian architect visiting
Cambridge.

Some Interesting Private Houses

Cambridge is possessed of a number of beautiful, well-heeled satellite villages which, together with parts of the City itself, attract that increasingly rare animal — the modern private house patron. Some of the more interesting have been gathered for the following collection. The approaches vary although — being Cambridge — the intent to make an intellectual point is never far away.

Salt Hill Bridle Way, Grantchester
Architects Co-Partnership (Kenneth Capon)
1959

A single-storey house whose character is created by the contrast between the two white rendered pavilions at either end (which contain the children's and the parents' living quarters respectively) and the central portion, which is entirely glazed and topped by a dark-stained timber roof. The two brick wings project so as to enclose an open patio or courtyard on the south front. The windows in the brick pavilions are set deep, the parapet above being left open forming a crenellation (which looks less like defensiveness and more like rooflessness). Note also the two ACP Cottages on Barton Road, Grantchester, by the same architect, completed the same year.

Salt Hill

Howe

Architectural Review

Keelson 8a Hills Avenue, Cambridge   *80*
Eric Sørensen
1960-61

This single-storey house achieved the accolade of *one of the two or three best buildings in post-war Cambridge,* in *Cambridge New Architecture.* The entrance wing next to the road contains the dining room and kitchen; it is linked to the main living wing by a long, book-lined corridor, off which open a nursery, child's room, nurse's room and a maid's room. All rooms are disposed around an interior garden court, into which they open. The main wing of the house faces south over the garden, and includes a large living room, a study, a sleeping area and a bathroom. This is the parents' wing. The house is dark brown timber-framed, its proportions based on the timber units which are used.

2/2a Grantchester Road Cambridge
Colin St John Wilson
1963-64

Very much a case of now you see it now you don't. From the street front it looks like a continuous colonnade of concrete blockwork surmounted by a relatively solid first storey. The formal facade belies the fact that you are looking at two houses, the right-hand one being set back and beside an entrance courtyard, giving an L-shaped plan: the architect (in one) and a University Lecturer (in the other). In proportion, the street facade looks foreshortened, and the absence of a roof — and the way in which the window embrasures punctuate the roof — merely emphasise this. The interior spaces — particularly the architect's double-height drawing room — are very fine. Concrete block work is used as a luxury material (as in several other of the houses in this book). The post-and-beam aesthetic, so prominent in the exterior, is carried through on the interior with an elegant simplicity.

2/2a Grantchester Road   Snoek

Spring House Conduit Head Road, Cambridge   *82*
Colin St John Wilson (M J Long)
1966

An L-plan artist's house in an orchard. The heel of the L is open, as though the walls of the building had been rolled back, from which a timber balcony and stairs link the first floor to the garden. A fine double-height artist's studio facing north; and double-height living room at the centre of the house, defined by round, timber columns. Unusual (for Wilson) use of concrete Roman tiles on the roof, as though the building were in the south of France.

Wendon House Barton
John Meunier & Barry Gasson
1967

Externally severe and uncompromising, this house has a spiralling plan. The noble, central hall/living area is delineated by four tall columns around which the stair/ramp descends from the entrance from which open all the other rooms. Despite the brutalist use of blockwork and timber, the interior volume has a luxurious feel: grand volumes are a luxury these days. The architects subsequently won the competition for the Burrell Gallery in Glasgow.

83

Burrell's End Grange Road, Cambridge
Patrick Hodgkinson
1963-64

A mainly brick house, whose south facade is cedar. The interior is split level, lending a tall, spacious feeling to the living room, effectively on the *Piano Nobile,* the guest and service rooms being relegated to the ground floor.

Rawson

Wendon House

Snoek

Brecht-Einzig

214 Chesterton Road

Water Lane, Histon

Brecht-Einzig

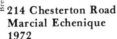

Brecht-Einzig

21 Horn Lane Linton
Yakely Associates
1971

A house on a long, narrow site, with a restrictive covenant preventing overlooking to the north. As a result, the house runs along the northern boundary facing south into the existing, walled, mature garden. The living/dining area is double height, from which a rather 1930s, Corbusian staircase rises to the upper floor. On plan the house is two parallel rectangles on either side of a main central corridor; that plan being obvious from the exterior. The combination of clerestorey lighting for the dining area and double-storey windows for the living area makes for a particularly bright interior.

214 Chesterton Road   *84*
Marcial Echenique
1972

Two-storey detached house, designed by the architect for himself. It is timber construction (à la Walter Segal) constructed by two men fitting all the pre-formed components together on site. The quality is worth emphasising: the finest feature of the house is the double-height living room, with stairs leading to a gallery and studio above. The walls are of timber-framed glass, or of fawn coloured asbestos-cement panels.

Houses, Water Lane Histon
Cambridge Design (David Thurlow)
1972

A clever pair of semi-detached houses entered from the centre, where carports adjoin each other and brick garden walls enclose that communal space. From the street side, a long, low roof with punctures for upper storey windows tops a quiet, single-storey building. The garden front is more dramatic, being almost entirely glazed. The real interest of the building is its section: under the apex of the roof there is a concealed upper storey, approached by an open gallery along the garden front, which contains bedrooms and bathroom.

Brecht-Einzig

49 Mingle Lane Stapleford
Yakely Associates
1974

Single-storey at the entrance front, and double-storey facing the view over the fields, the double-storey height being contained in an ever-rising roof. L-shaped in plan, with a top-lit stair in the re-entrant (a detail more commonly used in Scottish castles) the house has logic: main living, eating and kitchen area in one wing separated by the staircase from the bedroom wing.

Town's End Springs Thriplow
Sir Leslie Martin
1970

A tall, brick house whose rooms are arranged around a lofty, double-height hall — dining room, living room and study to the west, with a terrace in the dining room projecting over a water area, kitchen and service room to the north, and guest room on the east. There is an upper level gallery around the main hall, with the rooms following the same pattern as the ground floor. The brick of the house is carried through the interior of the main hall.

89 Barton Road Cambridge   85
Austin-Smith, Lord
1975

An introverted, single-storey house on a narrow site overlooking a small lake at the garden end, planned around a central path which leads from the front through to the garden. There is an enclosed courtyard on each side. Dark bricks, cedar windows and a flat roof punctuated by a pyramid rooflight over the conservatory. A house which deserves a hotter climate than Cambridge.

Brecht-Einzig

1 Old Pound Yard High Street, Great Shelford
Cambridge Design (David Thurlow)
1973

A single-storey cottage front with double garage and beautifully curved brick wall enclosing a front garden: behind a two-storey garden facade of windows or plywood panels in a timber framing, with brickwork flanking walls.

44

Houghton

The Paddock Stapleford
David Owers
1976

A timber house, constructed in eight months, mainly by two skilled carpenters. Set on a brick plinth with a central brick spine which contains the chimney, services and kitchen appliances, the rest of the house is designed as two rectangles around that spine. A slight change in level differentiates the public rooms facing the garden and the entrance from the more private rooms from the other side. There is a generous balcony at the upper level. The house was designed as a single-aspect house to see whether it could be repeated at high-density levels.

Edington House Little Eversden
John Meunier & Barry Gasson
1974-75

A single-storey, brick and timber house by the same architects as the Wendon House. Subtle changes in floor level following the downhill slope. Main living rooms disposed on the orchard side of the house — thus doubling as corridors — with main service rooms on the entrance side. Unresolved rooflight projecting from the flat roof.

86

Kirkwood

Throgmorton House Alwyn Road
Cambridge Design (Syd Furness)
1975

A house at the end of a cul-de-sac which has striking visual affinities with the maritime-inspired architecture of the 1930s. Here we have portholes, sun-decks and galleyways. The house is long and narrow, effectively two wings on either side of the double-height entrance hall.

13 St Peter's Street   87
Keith Garbett
1979 Extension 22

In-fill development with a touch of Keith Garbett's post-modern approach to design: possibly also the result of the involvement of the client, David Rubio, who is a musical instrument maker. This new brick studio has no private garden whatsoever. It is very vertical: the basement contains utility room boilers, etc., the ground floor, a wood store, study, and a studio for weaving and instrument making; the first floor, the living/dining/kitchen areas; and the top floor, a gallery, bedroom and storage. A general impression of 'Arts and Crafts' space.

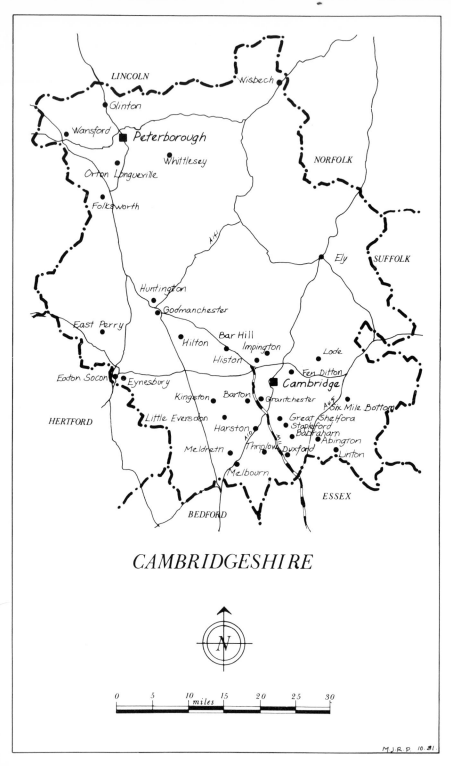

LINCOLN

Wisbech

Glinton

Wansford

Peterborough

NORFOLK

Whittlesey

Orton Longueville

Folksworth

A141

Ely

SUFFOLK

Huntington

Godmanchester

East Perry

Bar Hill

Hilton

Impington

Lode

Histon

Fen Ditton

Eaton Socon

Eynesbury

Cambridge

Kingston

Barton

Grantchester

Six Mile Bottom

HERTFORD

Little Eversden

Great Shelford

Stapleford

Harston

Babraham

Meldreth

Thriplow

Duxford

Abington

Linton

Melbourn

ESSEX

BEDFORD

CAMBRIDGESHIRE

N

0   5   10   15   20   25   30
miles

M.J.R.P. 10.81

EAST CAMBRIDGESHIRE
ABINGTON

Alexandra Studio

The Welding Institute Abington Hall
Staff Restaurant
Lyster Grillet & Harding (Douglas Harding,
Steven Brown)
1977 Rattee & Kett
Between 1957 and 1960 Hughes and Bicknell designed
offices and laboratories typical of their period. The new
staff restaurant is something entirely different: a steel-
framed glass box whose internal structure is made
manifest by brown-painted welded (of course) steel
'trees'. Bright contrast in the yellow-painted opening
windows and doorways. The building has quality and
panache. Some conflict between the visual requirements of a steel box, and the functional requirements
of a heavy-duty kitchen.

BABRAHAM

Architectural Review

The Greville Bio-Chemistry Laboratory
Institute of Animal Physiology
Colin St John Wilson with Michael Brawne
(Peter Carolin, John Greening)
1971 Johnson & Bailey
A rather mechanistic building containing laboratory
bays around the perimeter of the building enclosing the
service rooms and stairs in the centre. Large animals
are housed in the Animal Zone of the ground floor.
Two storeys: horizontal proportions and cladding in
Cor-Ten steel weathering panels. The gable with the
hoist is strongly modelled.

BAR HILL
The Village
**Covell Matthews & Partners, succeeded by
Marshman, Warren & Taylor**
1966 onwards

Bar Hill is a failed planner's dream. The intent was to prevent suburban explosion caused by Cambridge's expansion in population by planting self-contained villages at a distance from the city. These new villages were to have high design standards and were to be as self-supporting as possible. A change of developers half-way through the plan meant that much of Bar Hill — with the exception of the earliest housing — ended up as a second-rate suburb of Cambridge just a bit further out than normal.

Village Hall, Village Green
Keith Garbett
1979

Despite the formal composition of its gables (whose originality causes it to be in the book) this building is designed to be extended, and to save money, some of the finishes are being undertaken by local people. The split gable with its segmental and circular windows gives it visual punch. Clearly influenced by Venturi.

Houston

Bar Hill Village Hall

DUXFORD

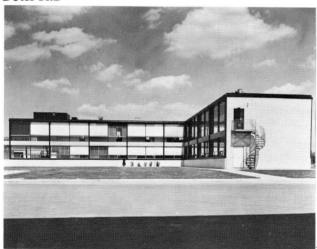

Arup

CIBA Development
Arup Associates
1959-64 William Sindall Ltd

A number of buildings by Arup Associates: the Araldite Plant, Research Laboratories and a multi-purpose building. The latter is a huge barn roofed in a series of arches of aluminium and glass fibre. The Araldite Plant is a large glass shed containing machinery surrounded by some single-storey buildings. The Research Laboratories are surprisingly neat and attractive: some gestures to the IIT by Mies Van der Rohe are evident.

Arup

48

ELY

Leigh

Branch Library
County Architect's Department (B G Lilley, D C Roe)
1972
A surprisingly graceful intruder into the Cathedral Precincts. A busy Branch Library with a truncated pitched roof and strongly vertical proportions. Brick. Civic Trust Commendation 1968.

GRANTCHESTER

Primary School
Cambridge County Architects' Department
1974 R Slingsby
Cambridge County have developed a style for their school buildings: purple-red bricks externally and internally, monopitch roofs and juxtaposition of gables. This example possibly more heavy handed than usual.

FEN DITTON

Musgrave Way
Cecil Bourne (G Gordon)
1974
Local Council development of single-storey houses and two-storey flats. Simply designed: white painted walls, nicely contrasting black timber windows and doors, and orange pantiles. A little bit too Mediterranean.

GREAT SHELFORD
House
H Redhouse
1931
A two-storey, L-shaped house rendered in white cement: the main entrance through a conservatory directly into the lounge, with a detached sun lounge beyond the garage. Very plain and rather lumpy. This house strongly resembles many of the entries to the Cement Marketing Company's competition for small house designs in 1933, most of which according to the jury, were in the *cubic flat roof style*. That indicates a clear contemporary perception that this form of architecture was as much a style as any other.

D

HARSTON

Snoek

Fison Pest Control Ltd
Edward Mills & Partners
1961
A notable building of its time; elegant two and three-storey block with elegantly detailed infill brick and glass panels. The tank on the roof accentuates the main entrance and stairwell.

IMPINGTON

RIBA

Village College
Walter Gropius & Maxwell Fry
1937
Possibly the most celebrated building in Cambridgeshire, the Village College was a pioneering building designed by Walter Gropius & Maxwell Fry for Henry Morris, who desired that local schools could double as colleges for the village out of school hours. It was the only public building Walter Gropius built in his short stay in Britain before going to the USA. Its architects and its function are possibly more important than its architecture, but nonetheless worth a pilgrimage. At the time of erection, the sense of space and light in this

KINGSTON

White Walls (house)
Darnton Hollister
1965
Single-storey, white-painted brick house opposite the church. It has something of a modern Cambridgeshire style.

Bakehouse Cottages, Linton

building seemed to herald a new world. Note also other village colleges at Sawston (1930), Bottisham (1937) and Linton (1938). Comparing Linton with Impington in 1938, W T Benslyn in the *RIBA Journal* noted that the fan-shaped hall at Impington required very expensive roof structures with little added advantage to the hall, and concluded *I came away with the impression that undue insistence of the theory of simplicity can very easily produce practical complications.* In interview with Gropius in 1936 John Gloag had ended: *It is clear that when Dr Gropius builds for the English, he will use modern techniques in concrete, glass, steel, wood and brick in a way that will be friendly to English eyes.*

LINTON
Village College
S E Urwin (County Architect)
1938
One of Cambridgeshire's series of village colleges which double as school and adult education in the evenings. Described by the *RIBA Journal* as *very pleasing,* it is a formal design with Art Deco touches in the banded brickwork.

Bakehouse Cottages
Peter Bird
1977
New house combined with cottages using traditional details with some care. Gabled chimney, garden wall and swept roof and eaves.

LODE

Anglesey Abbey Visitors' Centre
Peter Jenkins and Peter Inskip
1976
This is a fine little building, one of the best in Cambridgeshire and many times more worth visiting than other piles which sit more heavily upon the soil. A neat, single-storey, three-bay building which has all the precision one has come to expect of steel. It is in fact timber. The building acts as the entrance and bookshop to the grounds as well as a cafe, and the planning of the visitors' route through the building is particularly ingenious. By deft use of sliding panels and doors, and blinds, the spaces can flow into each other and into the garden outside when required.

PATS Centre Back Lane
Piano & Rogers
1975 R G Carter, King's Lynn
Another of the centres of modern pilgrimage in East
Anglia, this is the only development by Piano &
Rogers in the region. The building is cut into the chalk
on the south edge of Melbourn, all that is visible from
the main road being the principal storey or *piano nobile*,
beneath which is a parking area, decorated with
normal Rogers' glandular services machinery. The
building contains research laboratories, workshop and
administration areas, the workshops being in the core
of the building, isolated from, but contiguous to, the
administration section in which the researchers write
up their reports. The exterior image is a sheer, high-
tech box horizontally proportioned; that image is
carried through in the interior with its reception area
linked in glassblock, its yellow-painted cruciform
columns, high-tech demountable partitions and tubular
stairs.

MELDRETH
Meldreth Manor School
Architects' Co-Partnership (M Powers, B May)
1966 Kerridge (Cambridge) Ltd
There is some joy in seeing what is now called the
vernacular practised by accomplished international
architects. This school was the first residential school
and assessment centre in the country to be purpose
built for spastic children of the ages 5 to 15. Architects' Co-Partnership at that time were fresh from
designing Dunelm House in Durham, and had just
won the competition for the St Paul's Choir School.
What a contrast this is. It is a large development containing the main building, four children's houses, a
staff hostel, staff house, flats and garages, all in the fine

orchard of the village Manor House. There are all sorts of Scandinavian aesthetic predecessors, viz: the staff houses have distinct similarities to Jacobsen's houses at Sohølm. The buildings are white painted with doors and windows starkly etched out of the plain. The overall composition is one of jagged monopitches, the difference between the two pitches providing clerestorey lighting. The gables are elegantly designed with vertically proportioned mullioned windows somewhat reminiscent of Durham.

WISBECH

Branch Library The Crescent
County Architect's Department (R A Hodgson, G M Scott)
1975
Infill building in a curving Georgian street, the site of an old chapel. The new building fits well into the Crescent, but is marred by heavy oversailing second storey. The fact that this *clearly expresses the book stack on the second floor* is little consolation.

ourne

The Mary Delamere
Memorial Village
Cecil Bourne & Associates
(John Wisbey)
1975
A scheme of single-storey L-shaped cottages replacing existing ones, and conversion of former school into village community centre. Monopitch roof, black weather-boarded gable, white walls and orange tiles. Has the tranquility of modern almshouses.

NORTH-WESTERN CAMBRIDGESHIRE

For the purposes of this book, the area covered by Western Cambridgeshire is that part of Cambridgeshire County that was wont to be called the County of Huntingdon and Peterborough (previously the Soke of Peterborough). It is a relatively small, rural area whose main claims to fame are bricks (Flettons), the A1 (which virtually follows the western boundary), the Haycock Inn at Wansford and Peterborough itself. This tiny, ancient cathedral city has been selected for expansion as a New Town, in the course of which it has forfeited most of its former unspectacular charm. Development Corporations think big — too big to perceive the charm of alleys, courtyards and older buildings as an opportunity on which to build.

Generally, little outstanding architecture — with the exception of the Cathedral, Longthorpe Tower and Thorpe Hall — has come to this part of the country: of our period only one inter-war house, a number of schools, the modern developments in Peterborough itself, and an assortment of buildings scattered here and there.

EAST PERRY

Sailing Club Grafham Water
Robert Matthew Johnson Marshall & Partners
(K Bufferey, D Barrow)
1966
Three-storey, concrete building in a nautical, vaguely 1930s style. Some predictable similarities with the Royal Corinthian building at Burnham. Civic Trust Award 1968.

EATON VILLAGE Eaton Socon
The Health Centre
Bradshaw's Corner
County Architect's Department
(P Durne)
1977
Housing for two local Group Practices in a cottage setting: typical brick and slate monopitch roofs from Cambridge County Architects.

EYNESBURY (By St Neots)
Council house development
Barry Parker
1920
More in the Letchworth tradition, built as part of the immediate post-first war 'Homes Fit for Heroes' programme.

Gibson

Ernulf School
Huntingdon and Peterborough Architects' Department
(K A Sparrow, F Hall, E March, S Denham)
1972
Extended 1974 (J Woolmer)
Cambridge County Architects
(J Pook, G Parkhurst, M Ingham)
A formally planned school of linked pavilions.

GLINTON

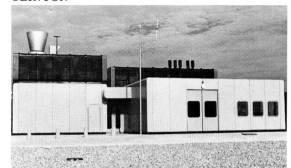

Gas Compressor Station
Architects' Design Group (R Perry, P Davies)
1972 Turriff Construction
An award-winning office and workshop wherein architecture is applied to engineering. Its scarlet painted metal pods are clearly visible from the railway from London to Edinburgh. It is in two parts: the administrative block clothed in glossy GRP-moulded, curved panels and round-cornered windows; and three machinery towers with their bright scarlet metal-clad tops. The landscaping is excellent, and the plan simple. The building was a vision of a technological future before that phrase became fashionable: fashions change so quickly that it now seems commonplace. RIBA Award, 1973.

FOLKSWORTH
Houses Manor Road
Ronald Quinn
1973
Two contrasting houses, one a stark black and white extension to an existing building, and the other a wholly modern building both designed by the same architect. The modern, the more interesting of the two, has a fine double-height living room overlooking a private garden at the rear.

GODMANCHESTER

The New Baptist Church
Silver Street
Whitehouse Design Group
(R W Whitehouse, R N Hackett)
Another double A-frame church with dark glass gables; designed to be built by the congregation, which it was.

HILTON
House near the Church
Dyson & Hebeler
1937-38
A rather duller example of a period '30s building: two storeys, projecting, glazed, semi-circular staircase, and strip windows. Possibly satisfactory in its rural setting, but not nearly as exciting as the stark, white and black examples elsewhere.

HUNTINGDON

Police Headquarters Hinchingbrooke Park
Cambridge County Architect's Department
(M R Francis, R G Stoodley)
1973 R G Carter (Kings Lynn) Ltd
A substantial development comprising a main office block, amenity block, printing block, gymnasium block, garage block and playing fields. Set in the park of Hinchinbrook House, the building was designed both to respect the beauty of the parkland but at the same time to assert its own character. The result is a series of cool pavilions raised on a grassed podium (with a hidden semi-basement). The facade has a satisfying entasis in its columns, and the detailing — particularly the stair tower — is very neat.

Huntingdon Library Princes Street
Huntingdon & Peterborough County Architect's Department (R T Ardick)
1971 Rattee & Kett
The Library comprises two main elements: a two-storey circular block or drum for the public services, and a single administrative wing with ancillary accommodation, all in multi-buff bricks, with lead facings above the windows, which are framed in black anodised aluminium. The drum dominates the view from both front and rear. Passing through the entrance into the public areas, one is made aware of an attractive, restrained but welcoming atmosphere.

HUNTINGDON
County Junior School
Mayfield Road
County Architect's Department
(K G Dines)
1963-64
Typical lay-out of the period, in yellow brick. Note also the **Fire Station**, Harford Road, 1964-65, and the Technical College, Twist & Whitley, 1963-65.

Diploma House Grammar School Walk
William Mills Headley
Headquarters of the Anglian Water Authority. An administrative development comprising four-storey administration blocks faced in white concrete, linked by red brick service and stair towers.

ORTON LONGUEVILLE

Huntley Lodge Special School
Cambridge County Architect's Department (T C Jones)
1974 Bernard Ward Ltd
Standing in the walled kitchen garden of Orton Hall, this day school is divided into four zones: a reception unit for five to seven-year-olds, a lower school for eight to twelve-year-olds, an upper school for twelve to sixteen-year-olds, and a general-purpose hall for use by the school as a whole. The three teaching components have been designed as linked pavilions, each one with a hipped, tiled roof. Above them is the mono-pitch of the roofs of the hall and the kitchens. This is a very elegant building.

ORTON LONGUEVILLE

Curlew Lodge Oakleigh Drive
Mathew, Robotham & Quinn
(R Smallwood)
1978
Eight two-person flats for the elderly, adjacent a shopping arcade. A straightforward solution on an infill site, surrounded by nondescript buildings of the '50s and '60s. DoE Housing Awards — Highly Commended 1980.

Walton Comprehensive School Mountsteven Ave
Dodson, Gillat & Saunders (J Robotham)
1967 F B Thackray & Co Ltd
An extension, more than trebling the size of the existing school to create a 1,400-place comprehensive school. The original school was the result of a competition in the '30s and was added to in the '50s and early '60s. The extension contains kitchen and dining room, boiler house, central library, science and arts departments, theatre workshop, sports hall and changing rooms, craft workshops, staff and administrative accommodation and music department. The accommodation is arranged in a formal pattern of one, two and three-storey pavilions, enclosing a series of squares. The architecture is 'classical' in character and very spare: exposed black steel framework on a varying modular grid, with infill of red-brown engineering brick and white asbestos cement panels.

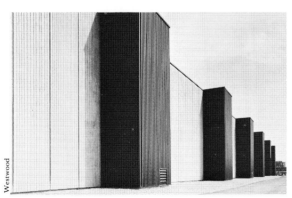

Westwood

Freeman's Warehouse Ivatt Way, Westwood
Scott Brownrigg Turner (A E Murray, K E Gilham)
1968
When built it was the largest warehouse in Europe, with about one million square feet of floor area. It has a steel frame with concrete shell roof. It is currently being extended in a different style by the same architects (in association with Court and Morpeth) the extension being heated by a scrap paper and polythene waste incinerator.

PETERBOROUGH DEVELOPMENT CORPORATION

Peterborough stands adjacent to the A1 to the north east of East Anglia, is on the main East Coast railway line and is unique in being both a cathedral city and a new town. Three separate agencies together with private finance have combined to create the new town: Peterborough Development Corporation, Peterborough City Council and Cambridgeshire County Council.

The Master Plan designed in 1968 defines an existing cathedral city with four new district townships at Bretton, Orton, Werrington and Castor, with Nene Park a linear park running along the valley of the winding River Nene and extending from the A1 to the city centre. Where valued, existing townscape and landscape within the designated area have been retained, such as the Cathedral, its precincts, square and adjoining streets and areas in the villages of Longthorpe, Werrington, Castor, Ailsworth and the Ortons.

The population has grown from 88,000 in 1970 and is due to reach 150,000 by the late 1980s, less than originally anticipated owing to government controls and the decision to defer the building of Castor township.

Within the city centre the Queensgate shopping centre, opening in the spring of 1982, is the largest single development, there are also a number of new office developments clad in either dark red or buff brick and stonework to complement the existing buildings.

Each township has its own colour identity. Bretton is buff and brown, Orton orange with buffs and yellows, and Werrington red.

Major developments are: Bretton Centre with the Cresset, a multi-function centre; the Bretton District Heating Scheme serving over 7,000 homes from one source; Orton Centre and Bushfield's School joint-use shopping and community facilities; industrial developments at Woodston, Bretton and Orton Southgate; Ferry Meadows Country Park recreational facilities in the heart of Nene Park; Werrington Comprehensive School and Centre serving the Werrington Township; and the considerable use of timber-frame construction in the many new housing schemes. The majority of buildings are by the architect's department of Peterborough Development Corporation (PDC) — Chief Architect of which is Keith Maplestone.

All areas are served by a new parkway network and a separate system of cycleways over 80 miles long.

Advance Factories
Maxwell Road, Woodston
PDC (N Stockton, M Crapper)
1976
Speculative factories clad in Alcan steel-framed panels, into which modular windows can be punched with little difficulty. The result is a streamlined image for units which can change easily as use dictates.

Aragon Court City Road
PDC (M Crapper, P Hewitt, R McKill)
1980
Speculative offices fairly near to the centre, enclosing an inner court. Oversailing of the lower storeys by the upper, the whole punctuated by brick columns, giving a squashed appearance.

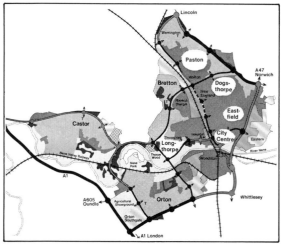

There is considerable emphasis on landscaping throughout the developments providing present and future citizens good homes in safe surroundings with generous means for the enjoyment of leisure and in an environment with a strong economy.

Housing, Pittneys Paston
PDC (M Highfield, G Walker, D Merga)
1975
Ninety houses for sale, each to Parker Morris standards. They are planned around single-access courtyards which—for garage forecourts—are pleasantly planned and well landscaped. It is a neat touch to twin two semi-detached garages under a single pediment: though more might have been made of the opportunity thus created.

Orton A1 Housing Stagsden, Orton Goldhay
PDC (G Walker, R Harding)
1979
Large development of timber-framed houses and flats, broken down into small clusters of houses facing semi-private open spaces. Notable for taking advantage of new thought in traffic layouts, with the longest of narrow 'moving' roads mixed with that of 'parking' roads which become lanes. House fenestration of some interest and elegance.

Sodastream Factory Marley Way
PDC (N Stockton)
1981
A purpose-designed factory housing production of soft-drink machines and equipment. Effectively a simple brick box with a ribbed metal fascia. The steel frame stands proud of the walls (as in Rank Precision, Loughton, Essex) and the entrance and offices are cut away from the brick and clad in glass.

Sodastream factory

Queensgate Shopping Centre
PDC (K Maplestone)
1982
Major heart surgery in central Peterborough, like inserting an elephant's heart into a sloth. The shopping centre engulfs former backlands and alleyways between Westgate and Queen Street. Doubts are more social than architectural — over the problem of a single-line development; over the closure of historic passages; over the loss of possible town centre residential accommodation.

Grooms

Midland Bank Cathedral Square
Dodson, Gillat & Saunders (D M Gillatt)
1970 Hugh R Wilkins & Son Ltd
An extension to a fine Edwardian neo-classical building
in a prominent position in the town centre, arrived at
after a protracted planning battle lasting almost two
years, some dozen different schemes, resolved only
after the interference of the New Town consultant
planner (Tom Hancock) whose hand is surely to be
seen in the design. The aim of the design appears to
have been to create a stone colonnade of basically
square openings with curved corners, the large glazed
areas being set well back to create this illusion. It is an
excellent example of fitting in without copying the
original, although marred by the more distant view of
the lift and tank housing on the roof.

Bush

The Key Theatre Embankment Road
Mathew Robotham Associates
1973 E Bowman & Sons Ltd
From its site on the north bank of the River Nene, the
theatre presents a slightly squat appearance. Its
character is created by the pleasant brick, with its portholes, contrasting with the cantilevered glass upper
storey which contains the coffee bar and kitchen. The
roof is swept up but is cut short, in Dutch style. The
steeply raked auditorium containing 400 seats has the
intimacy of a single room. The other fine space is the
upper storey foyer and bar with its superb view and
coffered ceiling and articulated by a series of slender
columns. The building has a unity derived from the
use of a limited range of materials and has become a
successful local centre. RIBA commendation 1974.

Bretton Superstore Bretton
Scott Brownrigg and Turner (K E Gilham,
W R Court)
1973
In the heart of one of the new townships of Peter-borough, this building contains 40,000 square feet of single-storey shopping area, and includes other shops as well as Sainsburys. It has a steel structure planned on a grid, and there is considerable differentiation in the interior between various spaces and functions. The main external impact is of the brilliant white GRP cladding for the fascia which is just sufficiently distinctive to identify the building as not being a factory.

Meat and Fish Market New Road
**Peterborough Development
Corporation** (D Clarke)
1977
A dark-tinted, featureless glass box which now looks out of place in its multi-storey, car-park dominated surroundings.

Magistrates' Court Bridge Street
**Cambridge County Council
Architect's Department**
(K Matthews)
1977
Designed in what might be called Brick Development Association Monumental style, and out of place among the humbler seventeenth, eighteenth and nineteenth-century shops and inns.

Central Office British Sugar Corporation,
Oundle Road
Arup Associates
1974 Mitchell Construction Ltd
A square extension to existing building linked to it by an octagonal brick drum which contains the new reception area. The new building sports a double skin, with a sealed external wall: the outside one is glass, detailed with typical Arup sleekness whilst the inner skin is part glass and part solid. There are two storeys of office accommodation, the upper also containing directors' rooms and meeting rooms. The architects not only specified the location of paintings, but chose the paintings as well. The single-minded precision of this building is slightly terrifying. Would the walls break asunder if a Director struck loose and chose a Modigliani instead of the Modern Abstracts?

Broadway Court
Peterborough Development Corporation (A Innes)
1974
Access to this U-shaped, three-storey office development behind a renovated stone Edwardian building
fronting Broadway, is through an arcade between the
shops. The rear building contains over 6,000 square
feet of office space overlooking a tight, rather dark
landscaped courtyard. Offices are neatly designed in
brick, with planting troughs at each level. The plants
are obstinately refusing to cascade down the building as
originally hoped. The projecting staircase at the head
gives principal access to each floor. Remarkable care
has been lavished on what is really a backland development. RIBA Commendation, 1975.

Ingleborough Alma Road
Mathew Robotham & Quinn
1976 Bettles Building Co Ltd
Eighteen 3 and 2-person flats on the site of a former
builder's yard in predominantly Victorian residential
area, with enclosed gardens to the ground floor flats.
The buildings fit in well with the character of the street
behind the notable rows of chestnut trees. The bulk of
the three-storey flats has been reduced by planning the
top flats within the roof and by the yellow stock brick
and blue-black slate roofs. The buildings are set as
near as possible to the back of the pavement.

Midgate Shops and Offices
**Peterborough Development
Corporation** (J Hesketh,
B Pulford)
1976 Mitchell Construction Ltd
City centre prominent corner site,
formerly occupied by large Edwardian family store with arcade and a
public house and other small shops.
A heavy, monolithic brick and tile-
faced building, with a welcome
arcade at street level and large ugly
picture windows at first-floor level.
Mandatory mansard roof.

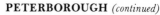

12-22 Towler Street
Mathew Robotham & Quinn
(Richard Smallwood, Philip Lavery)
1978
Neat infill of six 'starter' terraced houses built right up to the pavement: rather heavy brick string course and detailing on the front, the rear completely different with long sloping roof leading down to a single storey facing the rear gardens. A great deal of intellectual thought to achieve an approximation of what used to be achieved so effortlessly in the past: the next time, it should be easier.

Ashfield Thorpe Road
Mathew Robotham & Quinn
1979-81 A R C Construction
170 flats with garages in four blocks enclosing a large formal square of three and two-storey buildings. The architecture is formal and urban, with small accents in materials such as red crested tile ridges, purple slate roofs, the elaborate chimney ventilators and varied decorative brick panels.

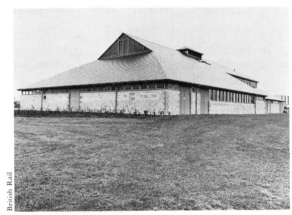

Railway Station
British Rail Architect's Department Eastern Region
(G Jelley)
1979
The stately early Victorian brick station was out of keeping with the new Peterborough. British Rail's new station has a certain glossy brittle, razzmatazz, with space frame and strong colours, although tank enclosures, overflows, etc. seem to be an afterthought. However, the walkways and platform complex are sub-industrial. It will be interesting to see if this new station will retain its quality for as long as the one it replaced.

British Rail Sports/Social Club Lincoln Rd
British Rail, York Regional Office (N C Derbyshire)
1978 Hereward Construction Co Ltd
A large building contained under a fine asbestos cement slate roof, cleverly sustaining volumes of disparate size. They include a caretaker's flat and committee rooms high up in the roof space, a large entertainment space with stage and dressing rooms, bars, billiard and games rooms and sports changing rooms. Inside, the finishes are hard to withstand robust treatment; outside fair-faced blockwork and pink timber clerestorey and doors tend to give the building a playful look, bravely holding its own against a setting of high and low-level motorways and a forest of lighting columns. Clearly visible from the railway.

63

WHITTLESEY

Sudbury Court Stonald Road
Mathew Robotham and Quinn
1977 Hereward Construction Ltd
This development of 32 single-person flats and
bungalows, 16 two-person flats, a warden's house and
a common room, five family houses, is to be found
among drab, post-war, semi-detached houses about a
quarter of a mile from the town centre. What a
contrast is this. A beautifully landscaped, inward-
facing development with warm red bricks, red clay
pantiles, no eaves and a mixture of roof forms. This
scheme shows a perfect balance between consistency
and variety: the house types and materials are very
limited, but there is no feeling of uniformity or
dullness. Allotments, a greenhouse and tenants'
gardens are all provided. RIBA Commendation, 1979.
Civic Trust Award, 1980. DoE Good Design in
Housing Award.

Herlington Local Centre
Orton Malborne
**Peterborough Development
Corporation** (N Butcher)
1979 Monks & Clifford Jellings Ltd
An ingeniously put together heteo-
geneous collection of uses, typical of
the '70s New Towns sociology. From
a distance, the intricate forms of tiled
roofs, dominating brickwork, stained
timber stairs, balconies, columns
and roof structure create a sense of
partly satisfied anticipation.

WANSFORD (left)
Standen Farmhouse Yarwell Road
Mathew Robotham Associates
1973
Nothing really to distinguish this
farmhouse from an ordinary house:
U-plan with mono-pitch roofs, patterned timberwork, portholes and a
good spacious and light interior.
Materials include reclaimed stonework, white render and an aluminium roof. Fine views.

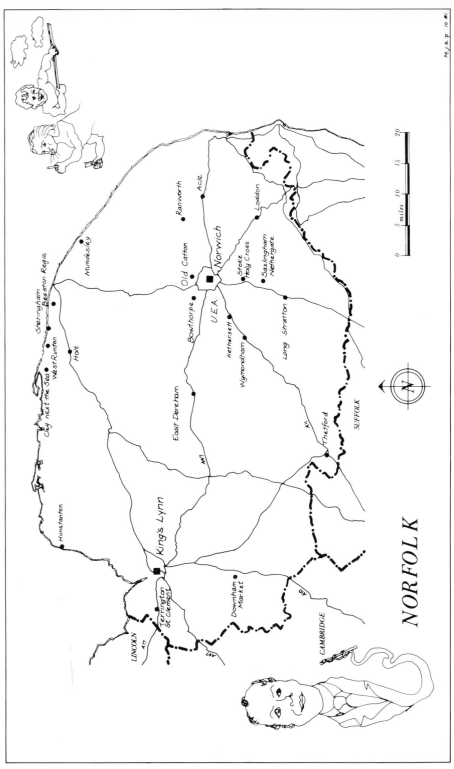

NORFOLK

NORFOLK

Little modern architecture of note was built in Norfolk between the wars. The occasional example of Home-Counties Georgian, a rare white, flat-roofed house, Norwich City Hall itself, and Great Yarmouth Pier about sums up the case. Immediately after the war, however, the first of a fine series of small housing developments was completed in Loddon, designed by Tayler and Green. Their semi-traditional yet plainly modern functional appearance made many subsequent Council Housing developments look unnecessarily ugly.

In 1952, Alison and Peter Smithson unveiled their seminal, Brutalist School at Hunstanton, bringing the county an architectural celebrity it scarcely deserved. For the most part, life continued rurally undisturbed — even by the arrival of the GLC expansion in Thetford. The principal talking point was the strange fondness of the Dutch for purchasing local agricultural estates. The arrival, however, of the University of East Anglia, outside Norwich, trailing Denys Lasdun, was an architectural event of the first importance, both for itself and for the heightened architectural expectations of the neighbouring area. Opinions will differ as to the consequences of the termination of Lasdun's consultancy, but it is undoubted that what remains of his vision is what gives the campus its peculiarly satisfying quality. Even the Sainsbury Centre would look less well at Essex.

In Central Norwich the City Council lost its reputation with its inner ring road and 1950s adjacent development, but regained it with a series of sensitive in-fill housing schemes at a time when high-rise was more fashionable elsewhere. The Civic Trust improvement scheme for Magdalen Street was the pioneer of that type of face-lift street scheme, as was the pedestrianisation of London Street.

In the 1970s this sense of innovation was continued by the gigantic repair, rehabilitation and in-fill programme in that part of the historic centre known as Norwich-over-the-Water, or Colegate. The scheme, titled *Heritage Over the Wensum* involved public and private funds and the creation of a new development company.

The Design Guide concept from Essex swiftly took root in Norfolk, and has produced one of the most complete realisations of the idea in the new suburban village of Bowthorpe. Unfortunately, Bowthorpe is not sufficiently thorough: smocks, organ grinders, stalls, Mangel-Wurzels, Maypoles and Yokels are absent.

For all the fine new architecture, little can compensate for some of the losses, possibly the most grievous being the wanton destruction of King's Lynn in the name of improvement.

UNIVERSITY OF EAST ANGLIA

Norfolk and Suffolk Terraces
Denys Lasdun & Partners
1964-69 Gazes of Kingston
The illustration is an old photograph before the completion of the Sainsbury Centre — in the middle distance, and the artificial fen which now exists in the rough ground on the left (with a pleasant new footbridge designed by Bernard Feilden on the inspiration of the Mathematical Bridge in Cambridge). Denys Lasdun described the intention as trying to create *architectural hills and valleys, in an evocation of the permanent human environment, and identification with nature and the primal dwelling.* The stepped terraces provide a transition from the ground up to the monumental teaching blocks behind. Note the typical Lasdun contrast between horizontal plane and vertical form, and also the Mayan influence in ziggurats and flights of steps up the sides of steep walls. The photograph shows how the result might look like on a good summer's day. The shapes are exciting from the front but are already proving rather grim from the backs.

Original UEA temporary buildings

Feilden & Mawson

(left): **The Fen, Bernard Feilden's Mathematical Bridge, with the University in the background**

The Sainsbury Centre for the Visual Arts
Foster Associates
1977 R G Carter Ltd

A shrine for high-tech enthusiasts — being one of the two prominent buildings in Eastern England designed by Norman Foster, this aircraft hangar-like shed combines two exhibition galleries, a School of Fine Arts, a University Senior Common Room, a public restaurant, a library, basement storage and workshop facilities, and a large reception/conservatory. The permanent collection is that of Sir Robert and Lady Sainsbury — ranging from primitives to paintings by Francis Bacon. The interior glows in a combination of grey and gun-metal colours, although the two mezzanines have a horizontality which does not seem integrated into the overall concept of the building. The entrance across a glass bridge at upper level and down a spiral staircase is particularly dramatic. Otherwise the principal features are those of high technology — the interchangeability of panels, the integration of the services and the methods of solar control. As a whole, the building's relationship to the nearby ziggurats of Sir Denys Lasdun is highly questionable. There must be more to the exterior of a building than the sleek enclosure of space.

Offices, Norwich, for Sun Life Assurance—Architects,
Chaplin & Farrant, Norwich.

EAST ANGLIAN LANDMARKS

By

BUSH

Founded in 1926 by the father of the present Chairman, this well-known Norfolk Company contributed a number of major landmarks to the East Anglian scene.

The Company remains largely in the ownership of the original founding family and prides itself on still giving old-fashioned Norfolk craftsmanship —sometimes handed down over three generations in the Company, and including the comparatively rare craft of Norfolk Flint Walling among others.

The combination of fine craftsmanship and expert management has led to a number of Civic Trust and individual Craft Awards being made, whilst the personal interest of the Directors creates a solid feeling of confidence in the minds of building owners.

Operating throughout East Anglia the Company has specialist maintenance, decorating, joinery, farm services and small works divisions in addition to its main contracting activities which include every possible type of building from the individual private house to a town centre complex.

King's Lynn Town Centre development for Norwich Union—Architects, Feilden & Mawson, Norwich.

BUSH

BUILDERS
(NORWICH) LTD.

MILE CROSS LANE,
NORWICH

TELEPHONE 0603/46326

Feilden & Mawson
Science Block

Restaurant and Forum

Brecht-Einzig

Feilden & Mawson

Senate House

Feilden & Mawson

The Music School
Arup Associates
1973 Bush Builders Ltd

From the outside, the Music School would scarcely warrant a second glance unless one were looking for it: constructed in good blockwork, the same as (if not slightly better than) the rest of the University development, it would look like an appendage to the remainder. Once inside, there is a quite different clarity of thought. Although a small building, it is divided simply into a number of rooms for teaching practising and performing music on one side of a sloping corridor, with a fine double height recital room and recording studio on the other. The slope is exploited to give different heights and acoustic volumes for the various practice and teaching rooms. Articulation in the corridor is achieved by projecting porches to each practice room, for sound deadening purposes, and the multi-coloured sound baffles hanging from the ceiling.

Other Buildings

A number of architects have been involved with UEA, including Peter Barefoot and Partners, Johns Slater and Haward, and Edward Skipper and Associates. Although their buildings do not have the same purity as those of Lasdun or Arup, it is remarkable how coherent the campus remains.

Of those other architects, by far the most prominent are **Feilden and Mawson** who had been responsible for the pre-Lasdun temporary buildings. Their work includes the library extension (1972). The Medical centre (1973) Chaplaincy (1971) Forum (1972) Restaurant (1971) and science block (1973). Their buildings, within this hard style, are more formal than usual. Given that context, the Italian-seeming forum is something of a success.

City Hall St Peter's Street
C H James and S Rowland Pierce
1938
This competition-winning town hall is Scandinavian in appearance: asymmetrical tower at the northern end, clock fixed directly on to the brickwork, brick with stone banding and a great, bare portico reaching down to the first storey. It is a very large development, enclosing three sides of a square, whose interiors are as modern as the exterior. For all that, it is over-scaled in relation to the Guild Hall, and foreshadows its more anonymous imitators of post-war. The second prize was given to Sir John Burnet, Tait & Lorne, with an even more undigested version of their Scottish Office scheme in Edinburgh.

Presbyterian Church
Unthank Road
Bernard Feilden
1954-6
Very Swedish-inspired coming only a few years after the Architectural Press published a book on the place. The tower is a variation on Stockholm Town Hall. Pevsner called it *Mid-century Expressionist.*

Office and House
71a Cathedral Close
Feilden & Mawson
1955
Touches of the Festival of Britain style: yet despite its modernity, it fits well in the Cathedral Close.

Norwich Central Library Esperanto Way, Bethel Street
Norwich City Architect's Department (J Vanston)
1962
The Library was designed to form the western side of a new square south of the city hall, with St Peter Mancroft Church on the eastern side. It is a big building, including lending, reference, local history and children's libraries, a periodicals room, a records office, administrative offices and a lecture theatre. There is also an American room which, together with a fountain in the courtyard forms a memorial to USAF personnel who served in the area..

Architects' own Office Ferry Road
Feilden & Mawson (M Rose)
1968 T Gill & Son (Norwich) Ltd
In its time, this small office block set back from the River Wensum was one of the more sophisticated modern buildings in Norwich. An essay in contrasts between the horizontally banded offices in a pleasant brown brick, and the verticality of the service tower. Flanked by two pleasant Edwardian houses, the building stands well: it would lose some of its interest without such contrasts. Civic Trust Award.

64/90 Pottergate
Norwich City Architect's Department
(A C Whitwood)
1970
Part of a continuous programme of good housing developments in the city centre by the City Council that has continued for about 25 years. This scheme of flats and garages is a good piece of townscape, filling in one of several open spaces needed to consolidate this street front. It also included the rehabilitation of a property in Pottergate — all that remained of the original Jenny Lind Hospital, and minor repairs and redecorations to Borrow House, once the home of George Borrow. DoE Good Design in Housing Award (1971): Civic Trust Award (1972).

21 Upton Close
John Winter
1956
A strangely classically proportioned house in suburban Norwich, built with local red bricks and a concrete roof. Essentially in three bays, it is placed around a brick case. Some clear pointers to Winter's subsequent celebrated house by Highgate, Coventry, London.

Lambert

Private House and Architect's Office
Trowse Millgate, Bracondale
Malcolm Rose
1970 W W Gould (Norwich) Ltd
A striking building on the edge of Norwich which faces across the bank of the River Yare to the island and meadows beyond, its mellow concrete blocks and stained timber blending with the colours of the landscape around it. The height of the building steps down from the huge first floor main office window with a series of lower roofs to mark the transition from the open-ness of the main road and the narrow private road beyond. The ground floor living accommodation was designed to change with a growing family. The double-height living room, with its unpainted fair-faced blockwork, timber ceiling and stained windows is a splendid space.

Housing at Camp Road Thorpe Hamlet
Norwich City Architect's Department (P Eccleshare)
1971
A redevelopment scheme involving public participation, continuous discussion with local residents, retaining plants from existing gardens, has resulted in a modern traditional scheme. It mixed people on foot with care well before the advent of the 'Mews Courts' of the later 1970s.

Eaton Hall School Pettus Road
Norwich City Architect's Department (Elizabeth Comrie)
1972
A school for emotionally disturbed children which has to provide a stable and reassuring background; the result is a rambling, single-storey building with an interesting roof line.

MadderMarket Theatre
St Johns Alley
Lambert & Innes
1966 W W Gould (Norwich) Ltd
The problem of providing a new rehearsal room, a foyer and a coffee bar to an existing historic theatre has been solved by leading people into a new corner entrance without detracting from the original historic facade. Worth visiting to see how this was achieved.

Food Research Institute
Colney Lane
Feilden & Mawson
(D Luckhurst)
1968
A large three/four-storey research building set into a hillside overlooking the River Yare. Contrast between the long rectangular blocks, the rolling hillside, and the verticality of the central service tower and chimney.

Beechbank Unthank Road
Furze & Hayden
1969
High-density scheme of 20 houses and 20 flats, quite advanced for its period in 1969. The buildings are arranged round a pleasant, well landscaped inner quadrangle.

GGS
Odeon Cinema, Anglia Square

Anglia Square
Alan Cooke Associates
1972
Anglia Square is a successful shopping square adjacent to the new HMSO offices in red brick and glass. It might be worth looking at the painted concrete, 1,200-seater Odeon Cinema. Generally, the development is out of scale for Norwich and has a sub-Metropolitan character. The City Planning Department has accepted the need to expand this development to cater for large multiple stores.

British Red Cross HQ
Coronation Road, Hellesdon
Feilden & Mawson
(Marshall Hopkins)
1969 Bush Builders Ltd
Offices, library, conference hall and garage, all in a brick and timber building of studied geometrics.

Lower School Bishopgate
Feilden & Mawson (J C Browning)
1971
Small, brown brick, single-storey group of pavilions planned as group teaching areas on the edge of a playing field.

Eaton Old Hall Hurd Road
Edward Skipper and Associates
(B Henderson, M Bain, M Calvert)
1971-4
A development of houses and flats surrounding an historic building, which won a DOE Housing Award in 1975. The spaces are designed to create the atmosphere of college courtyards. The houses are neat, unassertive, yet have adequate presence in this historic setting.

Cornish

Norfolk Tower Surrey Street
Furze & Hayden (J Cubitt)
1972 R G Carter Ltd
Norwich has its share of undistinguished office blocks, and it is worth drawing attention to Norfolk Tower as a building which is more prominent than most and also better designed. It is in two parts, one of three storeys facing the road in an attempt to continue the scale of the existing street; with a 10-storey block behind. The reinforced concrete which articulates each floor on the tower contains red/brown aggregate in an attempt to merge with existing local colour. The entire structure is in reinforced concrete, with exposed vertical shuttering as was the fashion of the time. The planners are responsible for deciding whether such a tower should or should not be built: but given that it was permitted, at least this one has a certain strength of character.

Queen Elizabeth Close Palace Plain
Feilden & Mawson (Simon Crosse, C Garner)
1973 W W Gould (Norwich) Ltd
A fine scheme of sheltered flats for the WRVS on a site that was once the orchard for the Bishop's Palace. The flats all face into the centre of the site, which is richly landscaped with brick fountains, timber pergola, and good planting. Excellent and imaginative use is made of an existing flint wall at the rear, distinguished by a tall dormer window which illustrates the access to the first floor. Emergency escape from the first floor access is provided by a new flint drum tower at the end of that wall. The scheme has well deserved its various awards which include a RIBA Commendation.

St Peters House 23 Cattle Market Street
Elsom Pack Roberts (Keith Blowers)
1975 R G Carter Ltd
Probably one of the best examples of modern office infill in Eastern England. It is designed so that from the street it looks like two pavilions of differing heights, which is explained by the fact that the right-hand pavilion is in fact the gable of a fairly long office development going back from the road. Some very neat brick details — including quoins (largely invisible except close up) good paving, string-courses and a general crispness.

Elaine Herbert House Prior Court,
The Great Hospital, Bishopgate
Wearing Hastings & Rossi (A P Rossi)
1973
Wearing Hastings & Brooks (T W Norton)
1979

Two separate new buildings for residential occupation by the elderly (the Great Hospital's traditions go back to 1249) in an outstanding setting separated by six years. The rather clumsily outlined, deep-set inverted bay windows (serving three rooms each) emphasise the squat proportions of the earlier. The later adopts the neo-Dutch form of an existing building. Interesting within the Norwich context to see an alternative to the neo-vernacular being practised everywhere else.

Wood

Queen Anne Yard Colegate
Michael & Sheila Gooch
1975

A restoration of some sixteenth- and seventeenth-century buildings, with a new corner block to replace those that fell down. Nice restoration, a sympathetic scale, rather crude brick arches over windows, and horizontal dormers in the roof. *Note:* This scheme forms part of the much wider scheme of restoration and infill in the historic Colegate area of Norwich, which is worth an extended visit.

Studio House Mile End Close
Michael Calvert
1975
An architect's house at the end of a large garden noted for its jagged profile, partly caused by the gallery within the living room.

78

Luckhurst

Friars Quay Colegate
Feilden & Mawson (D Luckhurst, R Thompson)
1975 John Youngs Ltd
A redevelopment of a derelict, former industrial site in the very heart of Norwich on the banks of the River Wensum — and surrounded on three of its sides by historic buildings. The scheme is the result of a partnership between a private developer and a City Council to build houses for sale. High density, leading to a terraced form of three and four-storey houses. Individual houses identified by not very subtle changes in the colour of the brickwork, and in differing heights between groups of buildings. General character is one of red brick and red pantiles, appearance being 'Maltings' style (helped by the chimneys) once again of a Baltic character.

Elliot House Ber Street
Edward Skipper and Associates (D Cooper)
1975 Bush Builders
A four-storey office block whose design conceals its bulk. A second storey is jettied out in a rather precious imitation of the sixteenth-century building across the street, whilst the top storey is recessed back behind a glazed clerestorey. The lift shaft is rather over-dominant. It would have suited historic Norwich better, were it not so aggressively free standing.

Cornish

Phase III Housing, Camp Road Ladbroke Place
Tayler & Green (G Ling)
1976
It would not be unfair to call this Tayler & Green's last
scheme (see Norfolk Introduction, and *Loddon,*
page 88). They have come a long way from the
austerity of their original buildings for Loddon. The
scheme consists of 87 flats, some shops, garages and
open parking, on one of the highest areas with views
over the entire city. The architects have responded to
the difficult site by creating what is, in effect, a
Hanseatic Square, more redolent of the Baltic Ports
than East Anglia. There cannot be too many schemes
in Britain with patterned brick, pre-cast flint panels
(knapped and un-knapped) and decorative
bargeboarding. Perhaps it is Eastern England's first
attempt at being post-modern?

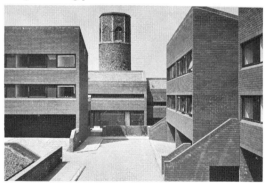

St Benedicts Housing Ten Bell Court and
Wellington Green
Edward Skipper & Associates (D Cooper, A Teather)
1976 T Gill & Son
Over 100 flats in the centre of the city, part of a
conservation area which included the round flint tower
of a mediaeval church. Red brick, making interesting
use of the changes in level, but in general a rather
chunky approach to detailing and scale. Duality
between horizontal strip windows and the verticality of
the site not resolved.

Don Pratt Court
Norwich City Architect's
Department (A E Wardle)
1977
A sheltered housing scheme in one
of the last clearance areas of the
city, comprising 20 single-storey
cottages, each with their own
garden.

Pockthorpe Development
Barrack Street
Lambert Scott & Innes (P Dean)
1977
Flats and houses designed around
three different courts of a former
brewery site. Another example of
traditional modern.

Norfolk Hostel for the Young Deaf
Lambert Scott & Innes (J Scott, D Seville)
1979 W W Gould (Norwich) Ltd
Tucked into a site immediately below the Black Tower on the ancient city walls, this consists of 15 bed-sitting-rooms, kitchens and toilets. The large common room serves as a social centre for the deaf in the local community. Red bricks, dark orange pantiles, dark stained timber, and a scheme which encloses its own community. Slightly heavy detailing for a small scheme.

NORFOLK COUNTY

ACLE

BEESTON REGIS
House
W F Tuthill
1934
Another little house, part two-storey, part one-storey, of cream rendered brickwork and yellow painted metal casement windows. Some peculiarities of planning.

High School South Walsham Road
Norfolk County Architect's Department (C Garner)
1977
Technically an extension to a school of little character, the new building lashes out with strong concrete and blockwork modelling, complete with gargoyle-like waterspouts, buttresses, and projecting bay windows.

F

BOWTHORPE

Bowthorpe is situated to the west of Norwich, south of the existing built-up area of Costessey (which is outside the city boundary), and bounded to the south by the River Yare. In 1973, the City Council determined to develop the area into a largely self-contained community of 13,500 people: a 10% expansion of the city. The housing is divided into three villages, each with its own local centre: **Clover Hill, Chapel Break** and **Three Score.** The employment area backs onto existing industrial sites and there is a formal park, for the benefit of the western side of the city to the north. The River Yare and its flood plain to the south form further public open space. The main shopping and social centre is established next to Bowthorpe Hall. In an attempt to ensure a complete inter-mix of all types of housing tenure, private, public, owner occupied and tenanted, housing association, sheltered, single-person accommodation or single plots, there is a rule that no single land block allocated for any of these uses shall be greater than 5 acres. Emphasis has also been given to foot-paths, cycle tracks and bus-only routes. Much of Bowthorpe is very pleasantly pedestrian.

More than 50 architects and designers working for some 30 firms and authorities have contributed, not counting dozens of technicians and engineers of various disciplines. In an attempt to cut out some of the more unfortunate excesses of twentieth-century housing a Design Guide was produced. Maybe it has been more successful in limiting the said excesses than promoting originality; nevertheless the task of co-ordination would have been well nigh impossible without it.

Clover Hill village centre on the highest point of the site and the starting point in late 1975, was deliberately designed to be inward-looking, focusing on the footpath/cycletrack network and turning its back on the East Anglian winds. **Chapel Break** village centre will be the reverse, open and facing a much larger village green.

Although the first village is almost complete, the first phases of the main centre and the employment area established, the formal park in use, the infrastructure for the second village substantially constructed and thousands of trees planted, it is now obvious that the original estimate of 10 years for completion is going to be considerably exceeded.

Sainsbury Supermarket
Sainsbury Architects' Department Z-plan Tithe Barn complex with a nicely swept roof.

Clover Hill Flats
Edward Skipper and Associates
The crunch: high-density vernacular: spot the pantiles.

Bowthorpe Park Pavilion
Norwich City Architects (D Stead)
This building would not look out of place in Stewartby.

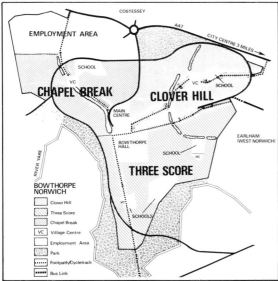

BOWTHORPE
NORWICH

- Clover Hill
- Three Score
- Chapel Break
- VC Village Centre
- Employment Area
- Park
- Footpath/Cycletrack
- Bus Link

Kirkwood

Kirkwood

Kirkwood

Bowthorpe Centre. Norwich City Architects (D Stead)
The vernacular image (before landscaping set in).

Brampton Court Bowthorpe
Cleary & Associates
1977
Private housing scheme designed as a London Mews
around two courtyards. Typical Cleary angular roof-
lights distinguish this from the rest of Bowthorpe.

CLEY NEXT THE SEA

House Extension
John Winter
1976
A house extension with a difference: a completely separate glass-gabled pavilion perched on top of the garage. A delightful *jeu d'esprit* from an otherwise rectangular and unrepentant modernist Norfolk architect exiled in London.

DOWNHAM MARKET

Cornish

Hillcrest First and Middle Schools
County Architect's Department (R W Haydon)
1979 Goddards
First phase of a larger school on a featureless site. Cruciform plan, whose dark slates contrast with white blockwork; and buttressed, castle-like sports hall.

EAST DEREHAM
Theatre Street
David Summers
1978
Theatre Royal Surgery
Reassuring group surgery, high roof, pended entrance, and some neat details.

HETHERSETT

Lambert

Fire Service Headquarters
Norfolk County Architect's Department
(B Johnson)
1976

A James Stirling-influenced fire building in red engineering brick and glazed clerestorey providing a good, cheerful and functional building for the maintenance of vehicles. More — or less — could have been made of the roof extension at the one end: but it is unsatisfactory as it is.

The Woodside First School
Norfolk County Architect's Department (A Johnson)
1972-76

The school has a hexagonal plan, focused on a domed central hall beyond which are the class work areas, through the bays for practical work, to the quiet places at the exterior. The communal spaces have exposed roof joists and facing bricks; the quiet areas at the perimeter have ceilings, plastered walls and carpet. A formal, crouching architecture.

HOLT

Kenwyn house Gresham School
George Grenfell-Baines
1959

The only building in the book by the founder of Building Design Partnership, designed before its foundation. It shows none of the BDP corporate style here. Kenwyn, in particular, is vaguely classical, symmetrical, two wings, tall chimney stacks and a central cupola. Delightfully old fashioned.

RIBA

Hunstanton School Downs Road
Alison and Peter Smithson
1954
This competition winner was one of the seminal buildings in the early 1950s, considered to be the forerunner
in Britain of the 'Brutalist' movement. Alison and
Peter Smithson demonstrated that materials used in a
formal composition of cubist shapes could have an
elegance in their own right: the Water Tower is
elevated to the status of a sculpture, and the plain brick
and metal boxes with the glass facades are strongly
reminiscent of the work by Mies Van der Rohe at the
Illinois Institute of Technology in America. The
Architects' Journal felt that *in that this building seems to
ignore the children for which it was built, it is hard to define it
as architecture at all. It is a formalist structure which will
please only architects.* The Hunstanton School had
imitators, but is devoid of the humanity and scale that
might be expected in a school.

OLD HUNSTANTON (right)
Private House Hamilton Road
Spence & Webster
1971
A single-storey, Miesian steel and glass box between
two suburban houses in Hunstanton. The architects,
notable for their competition winning (but never built)
scheme for the Parliament Buildings in Whitehall, have
a reputation for spare utility — and so it is in this
house. The house virtually square in plan, includes
three bedrooms and two bathrooms. Terraces have
been provided both front and back so as to further blur
the definition between inside and outside — the glass
walls being aluminium double-glazed sliding doors.
The flank walls are concrete blocks. There is some
pleasure in seeing a single idea being done so
thoroughly. Note also **Seafield,** 8 Hamilton Road
West, by **Gerald Lacoste (1935).**

Dow Agro-Chemicals
Fry Frew & Partners (D R Preston)
1960 John Brown Ltd

Making an unusual attempt to reflect the nautical
flavour of its location on the banks of the Great Ouse
Channel, this building is the administrative block for a
factory manufacturing agricultural chemicals, and
contains offices, laboratories, staff canteen, library,
conference room etc. It is designed around a central
courtyard, with a spacious entrance hall at ground
level and a circular staircase. The main contrast
derives between the white ship-lap boarding of the
upper storey and the blue brick recessed ground storey.

Bespak Ltd Bergen Way, North Lynn
Industrial Estate
Cambridge Design (S Furness, D Thurlow, J Bland)
1980 R G Carter

Unique in being the only recent factory whose architect
was chosen by competition in Eastern England. The
result is possibly the best working conditions in a drab
industrial estate at North Lynn. Principal features are
the overhanging roof supported on a dazzlingly bright
yellow steel framework, contrasting with dark brown
asbestos panels, and tinted glazing. Seventy five per
cent of the floor area is used for factory production,
storage and despatch, the remainder being two floors
of office accommodation. Rather whizz interiors by
Conran.

LODDON

Gillingham

Tayler and Green

Rural District Housing
Tayler & Green
1948

One of the few Local Authority housing schemes to make it into F R S Yorke's *The Modern House in England:* and notable for that alone. This scheme is one of at least 25 schemes picked out by Nikolaus Pevsner for inclusion in his Guides, all by the same architectural practice for Loddon Rural District Council between the end of the war and the 1970s. The Loddon houses are semi-detached and in terraces, colourwashed brick with pitched roofs and red Norfolk pantiles. Their modernism is clear from the plain outside, the strip windows, and the plainess and simplicity of the interior — particularly the open planning. Compared to modern council house standards, these are palaces. In 1962 Pevsner concluded that *Taylor and Green's rural housing can almost be called **post-modern**.*

LONG STRATTON

South Norfolk House Swan Lane

Tayler and Green

Other interesting schemes include:
St Marys Row, Aldeby (1948-53)
Entrance Lane, Brooke (1952-53)
The Warren, Claxton (1948-49)
Kells Acres, Geldeston (1949-54)
Mockmile Terrace, Haddiscoe (1949-50)
Smiths Knole, Hedenham (1949-50)
Church Road, Burgh Apton (1950-56)
St Michaels Place, Broome (1955-56)
Windmill Green, Ditchingham (1947-59)
Forge Grove, Gillingham (1955-58)
Garden Side, Hales (1949-54)
Well Terrace, Kirby Cane (1949-50)
Kersted Green,
Hardley Road and
Monks Terrace, Langley (1949-50)
Mill Lane, Seething (1950-51)
College Road, Thurlton (1946)
St Ethelbert Close, Thurton (1949)
Whiteways, Wheatacre (1948-51)
Woodyard Square and Hillary Terrace, Woodton (1950-53)

Ditchingham

Cornish

88

LONG STRATTON
Branch Library Main Street
County Architect's Department
(A Clissold)
1980
Simple red brick square pavilion
whose pyramid roof is ruptured by a
large clerestorey window. Pleasant
interior.

South Norfolk House
Lambert Scott & Innes (M Innes)
1979 Simons (Kings Lynn)
How should one reconcile the needs of a major office
block, with a rural — almost village setting? These new
Headquarters for South Norfolk District Council have
the plan, function and appearance of a mediaeval
castle: the relationship of keep and bailey is clear; and
it is, after all, the centre of local tax gathering, alms
and administration. All it lacks is a chapel and
prominent gatehouse. The dominant feature is a two-
storey services building in which the very soft red brick
and blue engineering quoins are seen to their best
effect. The remainder of the roofscape — and this
building is almost entirely roofscape — is arranged in a
series of humped climaxes which present a particularly
defensive appearance, to which the matt black slates
contribute. The interior has some splendid spaces, and
has been designed to try to avoid the institutional
atmosphere of most Local Authority offices (*no corridors
no Kafka*).

OLD CATTON

Piper

MUNDESLEY

New Junior School Trunch Road
**Norfolk County Architect's
Department** (R Goodyear)
1978
A nice red brick school with
inverted gables capped by chimneys.

Garrick Green First School
Norfolk County Architect's Department (B Riches)
1977 Kerridge (Norwich) Ltd
A good example of some of the thought that is
currently going into modern school design. Effectively,
the building is a large, single-storey village school but
entirely lacking the historic association that might
imply. The interior is designed to give an experience of
varying heights, vistas, free-standing structures, and
the use of natural light even at the centre of a very
deep planned building. That is achieved by having a
cruciform glazed area over the main teaching areas.
The exterior is a composition of concrete blocks,
aluminium windows and a light grey roof: all sym-
pathetically scaled.

RANWORTH

The Broadlands Conservation Centre
Feilden & Mawson (A Maufe)
1976 Wroxham Builders

The only building in this book which can be towed away to another site without much difficulty. The Centre's aim is to interpret conservation for people who care about wildlife, most of the space being used for an exhibition, although there is a gallery to give long views for birdwatching. It is a timber-framed building on pontoons, thatched in a rather Hansel and Gretel fashion. In order to keep vandals at bay, access is over a drawbridge. It could be said to be a good example of the architects responding to the whimsy of the site (but no gingerbread).

STOKE HOLY CROSS (below)
Boscarne Norwich Road
James Cornish
1976

Architect's own house on a fairly windy hillside just outside a village in Norfolk. It presents a stern face to the prevailing winds, and a Torremolinos face to the sun, enclosing three sides of a square, the fourth side facing south remaining open so as to create a sun-filled courtyard. At that level the house is single-storey, dominated by a red pantiled mono-pitched roof. From the street front the house is an austere flat, two-storey building in blockwork — although softened by the construction of a similar villa alongside, linked by a broad flight of steps.

SAXLINGHAM NETHERGATE

Extensions to the Old Rectory
Feilden & Mawson (G C Barnes)
1972

The restoration (if not sterilisation) of a splendid Sir John Soane Rectory, with the life of the building relegated to two pavilion-linked extensions — the central single storey being the kitchen area, the slightly French double-storey pavilion being for the children. The angularity of the extension lacks the subtle curves of Soane.

Cornish

SHERINGHAM

Cornish

1-9 Seacliff, Vincent Road
P L Martindale
1936
A speculative development of nine narrow, three-storey terrace houses designed like a large block of flats. Now much altered — new windows, balconies filled in, new conservatories and an air of decay. Yet a fine, white rendered brick crescent high on a cliff, but rather plain for its seaside setting.

WEST RUNTON

Cornish

Silver Firs
3 Camp Lane
W F Tuthill
1933
A confident, two-storey, white rendered, L-shaped house, with balcony and loggia beneath completing the square. Its well maintained, sharp form glimpsed through the trees, puts its younger neighbours to shame.

WYMONDHAM
Library and Resource Centre
Wymondham College
County Architect's Department
(A R Towlson, C Garner)
1978
Odd to think this piece of architecture is in the lineage of Impington or Linton. Formal and architectural: the rooflight influenced by the GLC Special School in Bow, East London, designed by Bob Giles (see *Guide to Modern Buildings in London 1965-75*).

TERRINGTON ST CLEMENT

High School
County Architect's Department (M Sadler, C Garner)
1980 R G Carter Ltd
Designed as a series of pavilions linked by covered walkways. The play of gables and tiled roofs, and particularly the windows in the hips, gives the building a villagey appearance. Perhaps it denotes a new style for low-level Fenland Schools, 'Norfolk snug'. Compare to West Flegg Middle School at Martham (1977) whose architecture is 'Norfolk agricultural'.

THETFORD

GLC Expanded Town, Thetford
The problem with Thetford is that it is really an expanded village with large amounts of new housing and industrial estates on the periphery. The shattered ruins of the mediaeval priory are worth a visit, as are some of the factories and housing developments as being typical of their period, e.g. the Graham Enock Factory (1963). Abbey Farm is a late 1960s early '70s scheme of terraced housing; Red Castle Furze Estate is neatly designed in a semi-rural, urban tradition, a mixture of mono-pitch and double-pitch, around courtyards (it is nice to see chimneys again); and the town centre pedestrianisation scheme by Peter Barefoot won an Award. Perhaps not worthy of a detour, but in times to come (when expanded towns are merely a memory) probably worth a pause between Norwich and Cambridge.

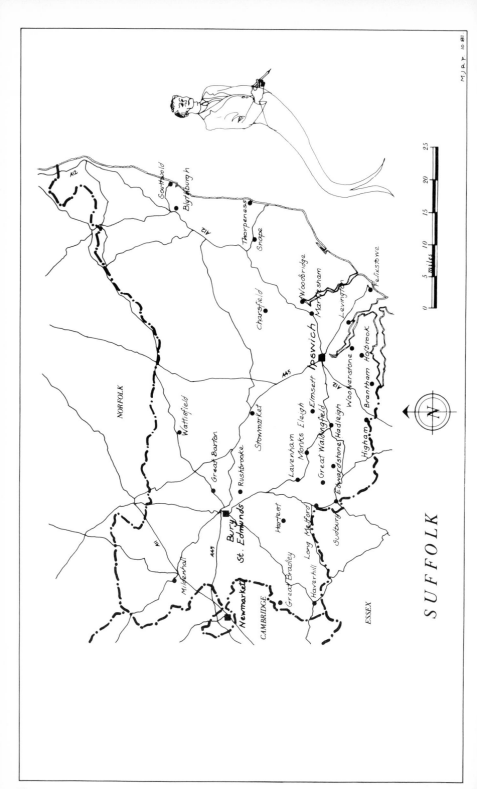

SUFFOLK

SUFFOLK

The modern county of Suffolk is the result of the
amalgamation of the two former counties of West
Suffolk, based at Bury St Edmunds, and East Suffolk
based at Ipswich. It is mainly prosperous, conservative,
and agricultural, with a formerly expanding boom area
around Ipswich. Few modern buildings of note were
created in the area before the war, with the exception
of the extraordinary holiday village at Thorpeness, the
wonderfully grand Royal Hospital School at Holbrook,
and Raymond Erith's Felixstowe Church.

Ipswich

The principal changes in post-war Ipswich were moti-
vated by the Town Clerk's desire to emulate the
Metropolis. The Civic Drive exemplifies all the
advantages and disadvantages of that philosophy. The
Greyfriars Centre is partially empty, and likely never
to be fully used (Edward Skipper and Partners). It won
the 'Bent Banana' Prize in a Straw Poll held on television in East Anglia for the most unpopular building
of the region. Opposite it, and reflecting its ugly big
face back at itself is the outstanding Willis Faber and
Dumas building by Foster Associates — a four-storey,
curvilinear building in dark green glass. Across the
road there is a series of high curved office blocks
produced by Johns, Slater & Haward, as part of the
new urban image. These buildings are substantially
better than many such commercial buildings, but still
look out of place in Ipswich. Opposite them, is the
competition-winning, early 1950s Civic Centre by Vine
& Vine. To modern eyes, it looks insipid,
unspectacular and urban architecture at its most
mediocre. Bullying its way into this complex is the
startingly red brick and over-sailing dark roof of the
new Wolsey Theatre by Roderick Ham, which
completes the complex. All these buildings are good of
their period, and some outstandingly so, ranging from
the early 1950s, the early 1960s, the late 1960s, the
early 1970s, and the late 1970s.

Cotterell

Gaumont Cinema St Helens Street
W E Trent
1929
One of three inter-war cinemas in Ipswich; the one
with the least interesting exterior but the only one
whose interior is in mint condition. Trent was the joint
architect with E Walmsley Lewis for the stupendous
New Victoria Cinema in London. A comparison
between this one and that shows the extent of
Walmsley Lewis' influence in London. The interior is
restrained but elegant; not Art Deco but vaguely
classical with an amazing octagonal dome. Well worth
a look. Robert Cromie's *Ritz,* 1937, and George Coles'
typical *Odeon,* Lloyds Avenue, 1936, have both been
converted into three cinemas, thereby losing their
interiors.

Rushmere Hall Primary School
Lanark Road
Johns Slater & Haward
1950 Kenney & Sons
Concrete panels, over-sailing roofs:
Festival of Britain Award 1951, and
style to match.

Lambert

The Spinney 108 Westerfield Road
Birkin Haward (Hans Fleck)
1960 G A Kennedy & Son
Large family house designed by the architect for his
own use in a splendid, mature setting. The house is
planned around a large double-height, open hall, lined
by a living gallery on the first floor. This central hall is
used to determine the layout of the various rooms in an
almost classical fashion. The building is constructed of
untreated brick walls, pre-cast concrete columns, and
thick cedar boards. Rather 1950-ish in appearance in
the way that the over-sailing first floor has a gently
pitched roof glazed right up to the gables.

Castle Hill Church Dryden Road
Johns Slater & Haward
1957 Kenney & Sons
Pitched roof, glazing at the apex,
and concrete patterned side walls.
RIBA Bronze Medal 1957.

94

Fisons

McCann

Harvest House Princes Street
Johns Slater & Haward (J L Harding)
1960 Walter Lawrence & Sons
Something of a landmark between the station and town
centre, this is an office block for Fisons (hence the
title). It has three floors designed around a hollow
square. The top two floors are cantilevered beyond the
ground floor and supported on V-shaped columns.
The floors and roof leaves a clear internal span of
40 feet. The structural and design form is unusual in
its use of profiled, pre-cast, combined structural
cladding units. RIBA Bronze Medal.

Hospital Water Tower Ipwich Hospital
Anglesea Road
Peter Barefoot
1961 V A Marriott
The problem was how to insert a building containing
water tanks, softening plant, incinerator, heating plant,
boilers, oil tanks, workshops etc, into a road of two-
storey suburban houses. The solution is an elegantly
designed vertically proportioned glass box rising above
a brick plinth which houses the boilers and tanks. The
skill lies in the proportion of the glazing of the tower,
and the fineness of detail. RIBA Bronze Medal 1964,
Civic Trust Commendation 1966.

Guardian Royal Exchange Civic Drive
Johns Slater & Haward (H Fleck)
1969 Vibrated Concrete Construction Co
The town's Chief Executive wanted to transform
Ipswich to a commercial city: the dual carriageway
Civic Drive, and these buildings were the nearest he
reached. Whether or not they suit Ipswich, their brick
curves have a certain Metropolitan elegance.

Halifax Primary School Prince of Wales Drive
Johns Slater & Haward
1970 A J Gibbons
A neat, single-storey blockwork and timber fascia school, one
of the earliest open-plan layouts. The assembly hall, physical
education area and pool are beneath a timber dome. Civic
Trust Commendation 1969.

Portman Stand 1 Ipswich Town Football Club
Hoopers of Ipswich (J Earwaker, J Lamming,
P Kievenaar)
1971-8
Double problem of providing protection for spectators,
whilst adequate view and shelter for successful football
club. Clean, no frills.

Clump Field Cambridge Drive
Peter Barefoot & Partners (Ray Williams &
Jeremy Buckingham)
1971 R G Carter Ltd
This WRVS scheme provides housing for retired professional
people on a relatively steeply sloping site, in thirty self-
contained flats, with projecting bay windows.

Donat

Donat

Willis & Faber interior

County Head Office, Willis & Faber Ltd
Civic Drive
Foster Associates
1975 Bovis Construction
A kidney-shaped deep plan office building, which follows the irregular boundary of its site with a sheer glass wall. Inside, the old concept of a central light-well has been exploded into a top-lit escalator well with exotic plants, acting as the focus of the entire development, and a demonstration of the openness of the design. There are two floors of open-plan offices; a computer room; a swimming pool; and a rooftop restaurant leading to an outside garden. The toughened glass is suspended from the top of the building. The entire development is an outstanding example of what can be done with a simple office block if the right client and the right architect get together. So well done in fact that questions of its relationship to the older parts of Ipswich can be overlooked. Foster claimed that the aims of the building are social, and the technology second to that. Willis and Faber represents a novel — almost American — view of how a large organisation should invest in the well-being of its staff.

Music School Woodbridge School
Bredfield Street
Johns Slater & Haward
(M Michael)
1978
Simple yet elegant adjunct to Victorian School.

G

Oaklee Stoke Park Drive
Johns Slater & Haward
1977 Sadler & Sons
Housing Association scheme of flats whose brightly
stained timber balconies which make it look as though
the blocks are floating.

Wolsey Theatre Civic Drive
Roderick Ham and Finch (G Parkinson,
J McCarthy)
1979 Haymills Contractors Ltd
The long-awaited new theatre in Ipswich is part of the
Civic Centre — but completely distinct from it. The
warm red brick, contrasting white concrete, and heavy,
oversailing, deep-eaved roof gives it the appearance of
a Bavarian Gasthaus. A building of such distinctive
character is greatly to be welcomed in this anonymous
area. Inside, the character is even stronger. Green
stained timber has been used delightfully for doors and
stairs, and inside the auditorium, the metal structure
has been painted red. The resulting effect is almost that
of recreating an Elizabethan Theatre — a Globe in
Ipswich. The character of the foyer has the cheerful
gaiety one more normally associates with Victorian
Music Hall. Well worth a detour.

St Edmund House
Rope Walk
**Suffolk County Architects'
Department** (P Brooks)
1980 Sadler & Sons
(Ipswich) Ltd
A County Council administrative
block housing architects, surveyors
and others, purpose designed to
replace leased speculative offices. In
plan, it is three squares with the
central one set back. Much play of
sloping roofs, tubular hand-rails,
and some penetration of light and
view for the upper floors to the
lower. Externally, a neo-Maltings
building with high roofs, would-be
buttresses and blind brick arcading.

BRANTHAM
House
Cedric Green
1965
Low energy two-storey house: the lower partially sunk into the ground and built of blockwork; the upper, with most of the best rooms, has a Douglas Fir post and beam construction, with timber bay windows giving superb views to the estuary.

BURY ST EDMUNDS

Police Bungalows Maynewater Lane
West Suffolk County Architect's Department
(J Digby, R H Stevens)
1968
Eight three-bedroomed bungalows: simple, white rendered, and a pleasantly designed setting.

BLYTHBURGH

House, Angel Lane
Jones and Dennis
1963
A home and guest house for Jack Pritchard, client for Wells Coates' Lawn Road flats in Hampstead, and celebrated furniture designer. Curiously nondescript from the exterior: a timber-framed box standing at the top of the site. The interior is splendid, dining room separated from the living quarters by a beautifully modelled chimney stack. The living room is almost entirely glass walled so as to exploit the view down to the river.

Wine & Spirit Store Maynewater Lane
Lyster Grillet & Harding
1974 R G Carter Ltd
A centre for the storage and distribution of wines and spirits on the slope on the immediate outskirts of the old city. Designed as a pure Miesian brown tinted steel box, becoming rather less pure around the offices in the single-storey projection. From the outside it has a spare elegance: from the inside it is relatively characterless and totally sunless.

BURY ST EDMUNDS *(continued)*

Greene King Warehouse
Michael Hopkins
1979
A new high-tech arrival in East Anglia, from a former partner of Norman Foster. This large distribution warehouse is raised above a flood plain, the height being used to enhance its presence: an industrial Farnsworth house, perhaps. All the tricks: flat roof, use of various metals, space frames, glass. Yet it looks disproportionately heavy: a flattened Sainsbury Centre. Intriguing glazed roller shutters.

Sport and Leisure Centre
Beeton's Way
Suffolk County Architect's
Department (H J Pieksma)
1976 Haymills Construction
A variation on the box: brick walls, with metal cladding above, made distinctive by projecting buttress-like steel members. The building includes two swimming pools, squash courts and the main sports hall. Its continuous canted clerestorey is architecturally logical, but functionally problematical.

CHARSFIELD

Delta
Cedric Green
1974
A case-study house: timber A-frame with conservatory on the south side. This is divided from the rest of the house by internal glazing and curtains. Not only cheap but elegant, comfortable, and a remarkable success in the passive use of solar energy which was the case it set out to prove.

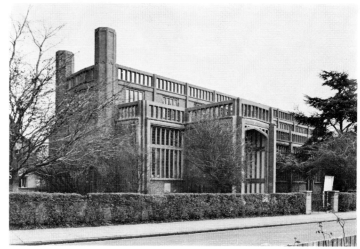

St Andrew's Church St Andrew's Road
Raymond Erith and Hilda Mason
1930
A most unusual church constructed of early reinforced concrete. Although squat Tudor-ish in appearance, particularly its concrete window mullions and the parapet, it is unique in Britain as a British version of Auguste Perret's earlier Notre Dame du Raincy. It is also a modern aberration in the corpus of Raymond Erith's revivalist classical designs (*see pages 120, 124 and 165*).

EDWARDSTONE
Private House Sherbourne Street
Frank Saunders & Partners
(C Huggins)
1973
White painted, horizontally proportioned house with double mono-pitch.

ELMSETT
House
David Brown
1973
L-shaped house with single-storey additions on both sides. The additive form, together with steeply pitched, pantiled roofs and rendered exterior result in a genuinely Suffolk modern building.

Commercial Studio

Sangamo Factory Langer Road
Johns Slater & Haward (H Fleck)
1964 Holloway Bros.
The first totally windowless modern factory in England, producing electric meters. A little conning tower on top.

GREAT BARTON

Matsudana Hall Park
Jack Digby
1966
An L-shaped, flat-roofed architect's house, constructed
of white painted bricks and a dark timber roof. It is an
essay in privacy, with long, white screen walls
enclosing private courtyards or garden onto which face
the glazed portions of the house. The public walls are
more blank. A very nice house indeed. Civic Trust
Commendation 1968. Note the Primary School, School
Lane, 1967. Nice brick and interesting piece of rural
expressionism with the water tank.

HADLEIGH

The proposed Headquarters from Hadleigh Bridge

New Council Offices
Arup Associates
1981 William Sindall Ltd
The centralisation of Babergh District Council Departments from various small offices into a new headquarters has been focused on a prominent site close to
the river, which includes a number of existing listed
buildings. These have been retained, and formed into a
courtyard with the new development. Suffolk pantiles,
orange brick walls and general scale suit the location
very well. Re-use of some of the internal concepts used
at CEGB in Bedminster Down, Bristol. The homely
exterior belies the quality of the interior.

102

GREAT BRADLEY
Sugar Loaf
C J Bourne (K J Wisby)
1972
A multi-level modern house attached
to diminutive timber-framed
cottage. White painted brick and
mono-pitch roofs. Elegant.

GREAT WALDINGFIELD

Church of England Primary School
West Suffolk County Architect's
Department (B Phillips, J Blackie)
1970
High-tech in the countryside. Flat,
space-frame roof, glazed clerestorey,
oversailing and independent of brick
walls. Civic Trust Commendation
1971.

HADLEIGH
Health Centre
Suffolk County Architect's
Department
1978
Single-storey, flat roof, brick build-
ing surmounted by wildly over-
sailing timber roof.

Brecht-Einzig

HARTEST

County Primary School
West Suffolk County Architect's
Department (J Digby, R M Stevens)
1966
A nice cottage-style school distinguished by its dormers, a dormer-like glazed gable, and an immensely elegant chimney. Emphatically *not* neo-vernacular yet it fits the landscape. Civic Trust Commendation 1968.

Upper Somerton
Frank Saunders & Partners
(C Huggins)
1972
Small, single-storey private house, with magnificent views. White painted brickwork, flat roof and heavy dark fascia.

Ketelfield
Aldington & Craig
1977 W T Wheeler & Sons
A compact steel pavilion located in and above a former tennis court on the edge of a superb garden. The form of the house is a direct consequence of the owners wishing to live in the middle of the garden, yet retaining the fine view: hence the height above ground, and the garden room which itself opens out into the garden. The house floats above the ground making it seem less substantial than it is. The lower, storage storey is invisible usually behind ranks of stored logs. The steel members seem disproportionately heavy for this scale of house, and the projecting chimney above the flat roof is unresolved.

HAVERHILL

GLC

Major extensions to Haverhill occurred under the Town Expansion Scheme by the **London County Council** and **Greater London Council.** Schemes of interest include housing at Chalkstone, Calder prefabricated houses at Withersfield Road (1962), the Mansol Factory, which won the RIBA Bronze Medal in 1961; and housing in Clements Lane—which won a Civic Trust Award in 1965 and Ministry of Housing and Local Government Award in 1964. Other developments include the Provincial Insurance block in the High Street (Murray Ward & Partners); Glasswells Building, Jubilee Walk (B & D Hatcher); the Haverhill Sports Centre (Suffolk County Council).

Fairclough

The Royal Hospital School
Buckland and Heywood
1933 Fairclough East Anglia Ltd
The School formed part of Greenwich Hospital, and these buildings are the result of a little-publicised competition in 1928. This enormous complex consists of a traditionally planned main block linked to two wings by classrooms. The development also includes separate hostels, houses and ancillary buildings. It is astonishingly successful for a revivalist scheme, comprising details from Sir Christopher Wren, Gibbs, French Baroque, and the sea side. Its glory is the great central tower which is a scaled out version of a Wren City Church Tower.

Fairclough

LAVENHAM
Harwood Place
Saunders & Huggins
1976
A small rural housing scheme designed to match a vaguely neo-vernacular style with modern building construction.

26 Prentice Street
Adrian Palmer
1975
Infill development in an outstanding conservation area — pantiles, colour-wash, first-floor oriel window — yet curiously not a copy of its neighbours.

Martlesham Heath Village Not yet complete
A brave scheme to plant a new village on an old flat aerodrome site. Several architectural practices are involved including **Clifford Culpin & Partners** who did the Master Plan, **Peter Barefoot & Partners,** and **Matthews Ryan & Partners.** The client required an 'instant village' — an idea which has more to commend it than some would think. The real point of interest will arise when the first or second generation of owners will start to personalise their homes. Not quite every fifth house has the same colour render, but almost. The great central green will be the development's best asset. According to Culpin's, the task was to put as much traditional village character into the designs as possible without those traditional inconveniences inevitable in picturesque villages.

Suffolk Police Headquarters
Building Design Partnership (K Draper)
1976
A heavy metropolitan building in a dark pink brick with upper floors jettied out over lower. Nondescriptly commercial in style.

LONG MELFORD

Westwood

Long Wall
Philip Dowson
1964

A small, low-budget house set in fine rolling landscape.
Some neat tricks obviously derived from the Barcelona
Pavilion, in the mingling of indoor and outdoor spaces.
Very elegant, with a skilful use of white painted brickwork, and timber framework and the roof. A restful
house, and a strange contrast in form to Dowson's own
house at Monks Eleigh.

MONKS ELEIGH

Studio House
Philip Dowson
1959

A delightful low-budget, A-frame house whose interest
lies in what Sir Philip Dowson, recent Royal Gold
Medallist of Arup Associates, would design for himself
as compared to his clients. Altogether more human
than the mechanistic perfection that practice has
achieved. A full-height studio at one end is separated
from the two-storey section at the other by the
elegantly tapering chimney stack. The interior is very
open and bright, and the south gable is almost entirely
glazed.

LEVINGTON
Fisons Research Station
Johns Slater & Haward
(J L Harding)
1957

An early post-war industrial building of rather spare appearance.
Lacks the richness of the compost.

MILDENHALL
Swimming Pool, King Street
Binns and Charles
1972

A low-cost, brown brick district
pool, with regular external
buttresses and clerestorey light into
the pool.

NEWMARKET

Darley

Studlands Park
Ralph Erskine (P & K Tham)
1976 Bovis New Homes
An imaginative development on the outside of New-market whose purpose was to bring architect-designed houses down to the cheapest possible cost for the private buyer. The resulting development contains over 500 one and two-storey houses, and a number of communal buildings. The layout is roughly Radburn, with the now normal central traffic-free areas with the usual difficulties of nobody quite knowing who is responsible for the upkeep. The original semi-rural atmosphere of the estate is seriously harmed by the completion of the Newmarket Bypass. Particular, typically Erskine details are obvious in the brightly painted gables, the apex windows in many of the houses, and the tawdry plastic porch roofs.

RUSHBROOKE

Architects' Journal

Rushbrooke Village near Bury St Edmunds
Llewellyn-Davies, Weeks (M Huckstepp)
1955-64 F A Valiant, Harvey Frost
It is the sheer simplicity of this scheme that is so attractive. It consists of a church, 24 houses and a club building for agricultural workers on the surrounding estate. Irregular groupings of small houses around grassed forecourts facing an old well-head help to recreate the impression of a long-established settlement. The cottages are built of white painted brick with black painted window frames and slate roofs, and are linked by high walls to create a sense of enclosure.

STOWMARKET

Cedars Factory
Feilden & Mawson (G G Mitchell and M B Everitt)
1977
Do-it-yourself beer makers will recognise the name Muntona which is manufactured in these maltings, which pioneer a new process of germinating barley. The buildings are really huge sheds enclosing this process. Skilful use of colours — dark brown, red and gleaming silver.

SNAPE

Donat

The Maltings
Arup Associates
1967 William Reade
In 1965, Benjamin Britten decided to explore the possibility of converting the largest malt house at Snape into a concert hall for the Aldeburgh Festival. The aim was to enclose stage and auditorium within a single space for concerts and recording, providing a foyer large enough to create a sense of occasion without spoiling the character of the buildings. Far more is new than looks: the roof has a steeper pitch than original; a series of cross walls that formed the hoppers were demolished; the smoke hoods rising out of the roof house the dampers for the mechanical ventilation; and the lighting control room is cantilevered out in nineteenth-century style. The result is a concert hall of proportions comparable to the best European concert halls.

SUDBURY

Elizabeth Court East Street
Babergh District Council
Architect's Department
(Christopher Chesnutt)
1978 Tanner & Wicks
A Spartan-looking courtyard development for elderly people with a warden, constructed of white bricks, white mortar, dark windows and slates. The scheme has elegant vertical proportions, though with rather angular mono-pitch roofs.

Snape Maltings

Donat

108

SOUTHWOLD

Ford Jenkins

The Nook Primrose Alley, South Green
Brian Haward
1971
An elegant little box completed in six months. Steel
framed with hardwood infill units, the house makes the
best of the superb views to one of the bleakest coasts in
Britain.

WATTISFIELD

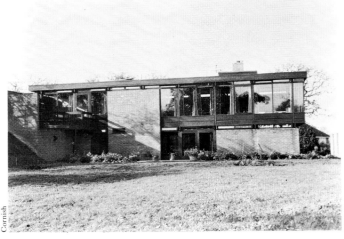

Cornish

Henry Watson's Pottery
James Cornish
1976
Another rural house following the fashion of a pavilion
on a piano nobile above less important rooms
in a brick plinth. The elevated living areas have magnificent views to the north and the east, whilst the
children's rooms downstairs have direct access to playroom, courtyard and garden. The structure is an
exposed, two-storey frame of Douglas fir with infill
panels of glass and a pleasant local red brick. From
some angles this house is very elegant.

WOOLVERSTONE

WOODBRIDGE
HM Borstal Hollesley Bay
Brewer Smith & Brewer,
with the Home Office
1973
Low-slung timber, brick and concrete houses, constructed by the young offenders themselves.

Royal Harwich Yacht Clubhouse
Peter Barefoot and Associates (A Gordon)
1969
On a splendid riverside site overlooking the Orwell, this weatherboarded clubhouse is neat and simple: first-floor viewing terrace, large windows and chunky massing. No portholes.

THORPENESS

Darley

Darley

Holiday Resort
Forbes Glennie, W G Wilson
From 1910 onwards

An estate village built as a holiday resort and described
in an early brochure as *the home of Peter Pan.* A combination of weatherboarded and half timbered housing,
with some unusual features — such as the two water
towers, one masked as a Norman keep and the other as
a huge wooden cottage — known as *The House in the
Clouds.*

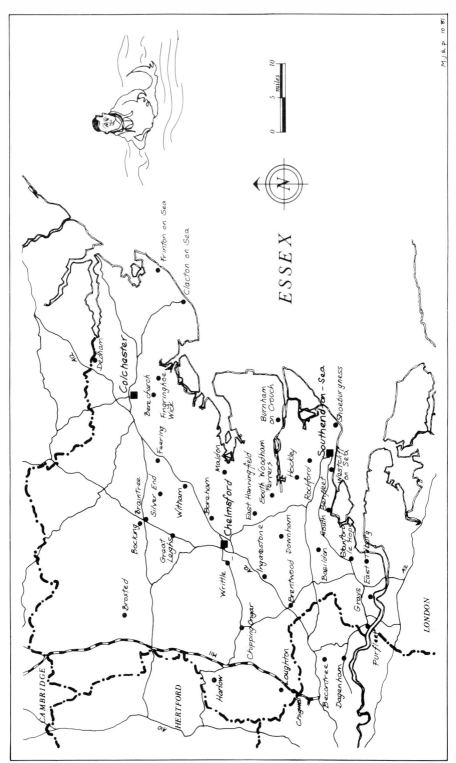

ESSEX

ESSEX

Essex is a peculiar county, vast in extent, with no natural centre or capital town, and with London remorselessly nibbling at its western boundary. The County Town is Chelmsford, formerly a pleasant Market town of little distinction; and what little it had, it has now sacrificed. If you stand in ancient Moulsham Street and look back across the dual carriageway to the town centre, the extent of loss can be gauged. Essex's only historic city of great consequence is Colchester, itself fairly drastically altered.

Essex is really a community of small towns and large villages — poor in the south-east, and wealthy elsewhere. The proximity to London meant that great industries (Fords) and estates (Becontree) crossed the divide and invaded the county. Development had already followed the railways into Essex, and it soon followed the roads — particularly the pre-war Arterial Road to Southend. The sprawl, for which the county became infamous makes it difficult to identify all buildings of interest. If preparing architectural guides is like looking for needles in haystacks, the Essex haystack is particularly dense. For example, Daniel Hoffman designed a most imaginatively stylish house for Pitsea in 1938, complete with curved windows, balconies and a three-storey circular tower. Was it ever built? It has not been found — but, knowing Essex, it might be.

The County has a reasonable selection of significant pre-war buildings, ranging from Silver End Village and BATA workers' houses through to the Royal Corinthian Yacht Club and the fun at Frinton on Sea. Postwar is lighter. In 1963 Greater London gobbled up much of metropolitan Essex.

The arrival of Harlow New Town and Basildon New Town were events of the greatest importance, the latter being one of south-east Essex's few economic bright spots. The County has been considered fair game for London's cast-offs and having faced a third London airport at Foulness it is now likely to get it, in the far more environmentally damaging location of Stansted. Another major intruder is Essex University, just outside Colchester: like the rest of Essex, it is just too near London to be entirely independent of it, yet too far away to make real use of it. Losing patience with the prairie-planning of developers' housing schemes the County Council produced a *Design Guide for Residential Areas* in 1973 — one of the most significant environmental documents in planning history. Although intended to tame developers' excesses, the guide has been criticised for being too restrictive on architects. Several schemes in this book — but particularly at Essex County Council's own hothouse of English tradition, South Woodham Ferrers — illustrate the theories of the guide.

BASILDON

At the time of designation in January 1949, the 3,165 hectares of the New Town comprised some 30,000 separate ownerships with 78 miles of unmade road and at least 5,600 sub-standard dwellings. Round the two stations, 3½ miles apart, the scattered development coalesced as a straggle of poor-quality shops, but no direct road connected Laindon with Pitsea. Of substantial structures there were few, though three or four isolated churches had a respectable ancestry dating back to the fourteenth century or earlier.

The designated area is approximately 6 miles east/west by 3 miles north/south. From sea level at Vange and Pitsea Creeks it rises to approximately 107 m on the south-west boundary which marches with the Essex County Council-administered Country Parks of Langdon Hills and Westley Heights. A more or less continuous ridge of relatively high ground links Dunton/Langdon Hills in the west with Hawkesbury/Vange in the east. This ridge commands extensive views southwards across the marshes and the River Thames; northwards over the New Town to the relatively open country beyond the A127.

Basildon has been developed in broad terms from east to west, the programme conditioned by the problems of piecemeal acquisition. The fragmentary pattern of land ownership is of course a consequence of the socio-economic history of the area. The Town Centre is logically located in the geographic centre of the designated area, bounded to the south by the Fenchurch Street-Southend Railway with a new station to supplement those still in operation at Laindon and Pitsea.

Industrial development is mainly accommodated in four zones parallel with, and having easy access to, the A127 on the northern boundary of the New Town; the last and westermost of these areas (Southfields) is currently being developed. The ridge of relatively high ground extending round the south and south-west boundaries provides generous recreation spaces and a Nature Trail has recently been established linking the golf course at Vange with the relatively undisturbed plotlands of Dunton.

At the time of writing, Basildon New Town has a population of approximately 100,000 (relative to a target population of about 130,000). Development of the last major industrial area is under way and current housing — now mostly for the private market — is concentrated in the northern extension of the designated area beyond A127 (Noak Bridge) and the north-east sector (Felmore). Consequent upon the programmed construction of a new feeder road south of, and parallel with, the railway, the last significant area for housing development will become available, on the attractively wooded slopes of south-west Basildon.

Raffoul

Chalvedon Housing
Ahrends Burton Koralek
(M Starr, P Murray,
J Hermsen)
A large scheme of 1,370 dwellings but which manages to retain domestic scale and pleasant variety. One and two-storey houses, each with its own garden, enclose communal gardens. Excellent landscaping. Buildings have steeply pitched roofs, and are easily adaptable inside.

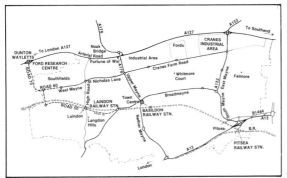

Laindon 5

Laindon 5 Housing (left)
Basildon Development Corporation (D Brewster, J Byron, M Naughton, C Plumb)
1968-72
The two-storey housing which forms the bulk of the scheme is based upon repetitive courtyards enclosed (by six dwellings) or partially enclosed (four or five dwellings) where these courts open onto the primary footpath system or the central open space. Courtyards are linked by archways at ground level and the exclusion of the motor car means that the whole area within the perimeter defined by the flats-over-garages is pedestrianised. The housing encloses a continuous open space approximately half-a-mile long and sloping gently from west to east; big enough for robust teenage games and at the same time completely safe for younger children.

Langdon Hills Housing (left)
Basildon Development Corporation (C C Plumb, G D Gentry)
1972-79
The Langdon Hills site slopes fairly steeply from south to north, with pleasant views, and the designers were presented with an inherent conflict between aspect and prospect. These opposed requirements are synthesised in the cross-section of the family dwellings. First-floor living spaces face south, while the glazed centre section of the staggered mono-pitch roof affords a view northwards. The fall of the site allows ramped access from the living room to the garden. The disciplined geometry of the housing terraces contrasts with the free treatment of roads and footpaths, designed to preserve existing trees wherever possible.

Langdon Hills

Laindon Health Centre
High Road
Basildon Council
(K Cotton)
1971
Large health centre cantilevered out of a hillside with parking beneath.

Felmore 1 Housing
Ahrends, Burton Koralek
Another large scheme, making an interesting comparison to Felmore 4 to the north. The houses are laid out in staggered, not quite parallel terraces, using existing landscape features, and creating a typical British picturesqueness. The terraces are short, and criss-crossed with footpaths.

Felmore 4 Housing
Basildon Development Corporation (C C Plumb, D Brewster, R Wilson)
1976-80
The district heating distribution mains are accommodated with other services in a common 'crawl-through' duct below the suspended floor slabs which imposes a spine-and-rib discipline on the layout. The rhythm of branching terraces gives either south or west aspect, with generous open space between the blocks. The basic planning unit is a court of 20 dwellings bounded by terraced housing on the south and west sides and containing both car-parking and toddlers' play facilities. Houses are timber-framed, on two or three floors depending on the number of bedrooms. Floors decrease in area level by level, thus producing a series of strong horizontals defined by the pantiled roofs with generous overhangs.

Pitsea Shopping Centre
BDC Architects (J Byron)
1975-77
Secondary town centre at the east end around an open market. Pitched, slate roofs, blockwork walls, horizontal windows. Good modern character, which complements existing buildings.

Raffoul

Whitmore Court Whitmore Way
Ahrends, Burton Koralek (C Rejwan, D Thomas, M Brown, R Burton)
1976
A warm and colourful scheme of cream brick flats and maisonettes — partially for old people — in rather drab surroundings in Basildon. The garden and landscaping are excellent, but the detailing rather disproportionate — particularly the heavy concrete landing, and gross orange handrail.

BECONTREE

Potter

St Mary's Church Grafton Road
Welch, Cachemaille-Day & Lander
1935
A most extraordinary, interesting building in brick, rendered on the exterior, displaying unusually elegant modern gothic windows, and whose interior recalls the work of Lethaby. The use of brick — particularly under the tower — is striking. Well worth a detour despite its current dilapidation and false ceiling in the tower. Interior brickwork clearly continentally inspired.

BENFLEET

Charles

BERECHURCH

Newberry

St Margaret's Church
Tooley Foster Partnership
1973
Prominent in an otherwise undistinguished district by virtue of its
great heavy pyramid roof, and
barrel vaulted covered entrance with
diagonal timberwork. Self-built.

Shipwrights Benfleet Road
Wells Coates
1937
An interesting house with splendid views over the
Thames Estuary. As a result, the main living accommodation is on the first floor, which is raised on piloti.
Reinforced concrete-framed construction, with brickwork rendered and painted white. There are metal
windows and external stairs — all the fashion of the
'30s. Despite the influence of the Villa Savoie as Poissy
by Le Corbusier, there is more on the ground floor in
this building than in the original: indeed the ground-
floor terrace is planned as an outdoor room with an
external fireplace. There is a sun terrace on the roof.

BOCKING
Howard Hall The Causeway
Sir John Burnet, Tait & Lorne,
and Douglas G Armstrong
1934
A neat building distinctive for its exterior: cream rendered on
a plinth of black glazed bricks. Plain windows, projecting
balconies, overhanging canopies — a refined version of the
houses at Silver End. Local opinion holds that *it looks as though
it were built by Nazis;* not realising, perhaps, that it would have
been deemed too progressive by the Nazis.

BOREHAM
Extensions to New Hall
Edward Mills & Partners
1970
The architects faced the problem of providing two substantial
additions to a fine Tudor building, one virtually forming a
new courtyard at the back, and the other providing an
extension of the main south facade. The result creates a good
sense of place, but the new buildings lack the conviction of the
original, and lacking a coherent parapet, tail off at roof level.

117

BRENTWOOD

Brentwood Place Sawyers Hall Lane
David Ruffle Associates
1977
Scheme of 64 private houses, in accordance with the Essex Design Guide. Too good to be true, but better than many such schemes with its richly satisfying materials. Infinitely preferable to speculative housing previous to the Guide. Winner of many awards, this scheme brought joy to the Council and to the developer who commissioned more, elsewhere.

BURNHAM ON CROUCH

Royal Corinthian Yacht Club Sea front
Joseph Emberton
1931
Three floors, the top containing bedrooms and an open terrace, commanding a superb view of the Crouch Estuary. Two thirds of the building is cantilevered beyond the sea wall, the building presenting a more open front to the sea than to the land — as one might expect from a yacht club. That facade is principally glass, each storey having a terrace partly set back from the lower. The whole building is an affair of decks and rails and sloping strip windows on the staircases: ocean liner imagery, and as modern today as it was 50 years ago.

118

BRAINTREE
192/194 Cressing Road
C H B Quennell & W F Crittall
1919 onwards
Historically significant, modern semi-detached and terraced workers' housing. Long before the International Style was conceived, these little houses were built of painted concrete block and had exposed lintels, a flat roof with metal balustrade and hollow porches.

BRENTWOOD
Broome Place
W W Wood
1935
Squat, L-shaped building with entrance in the re-entrant. Flat roof, terrace chimney, render exterior, and L-shaped window at the staircase.

BROXTED
'Hill Pasture'
Erno Goldfinger and
Gerald Flower
1938
A drastically altered, single-storey, flat-roof brick cottage with a covered way to the main door in a flanking wall. Virtually entirely open plan inside.

Charles

CHELMSFORD

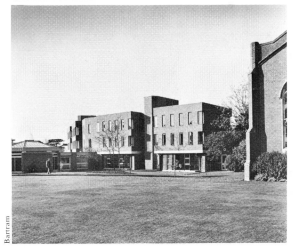

Regional Management Centre Danbury Park
Essex County Architect's Department (J Fulbeck,
G Beighton, M Gale, A Thomson)
1974
A residential and teaching annexe as an extension to
the Victorian Bishop's Palace. A two-storey brick
extension which curves into the park encloses the bedrooms, past two single-storey pavilions containing the
dining room and major teaching areas.

CHELMSFORD
Various buildings, The School of
Wireless Communication
Marconi
1938
Just visible from the train. Good
examples of their time. The school
is two-storey brick, banded
concrete, with fine curved glazed
staircase tower. The works extension
is concrete and glass of an interesting robustness.

Thriftwood School Slades Lane, Galleywood
Essex County Architect's Department (A Willis,
W Apps, D Kemp, M Mason)
1975
A delightful rural school constructed from white blockwork and topped by a dark grey slate roof. Well set
into the landscape, and creating additional delight by
its over-sailing roof to provide covered outdoor spaces,
complete with timber benches. Contrast Pitsea Briscoe
School in Basildon, completed 1979. White walls, tiled
roof, no over-sailing, with a different plan.

CHELMSFORD *(continued)*

Guy Harlings New Street
Robert Maguire and Keith Murray (R Singh and J Evans)
1979 Tom Green (Building) Ltd
Development for the cathedral around seventeenth-century Guy Harlings House. It consists mainly of Diocesan offices and a conference centre with associated facilities. Two distinct styles: the garden block (the Cathedral Centre) is low, white walled, with a pantiled cloister walk linked to the old house. The new street block is much more flamboyant — a three-storeyed, jettied building of rather heavy handed gables and lunettes.

COLCHESTER

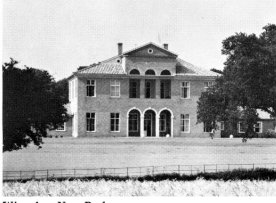

Wivenhoe New Park
Raymond Erith (with Quinlan Terry)
1961
A neo-Palladian villa of some interest. The entrance front is restrained, rather Sir Robert Taylor-ish, although it is odd to see the central pediment cut off by a cornice. The garden front is Venetian: round-headed windows and a first-floor recessed loggia whose arches are also decapitated by the same bloodthirsty cornice as round the back.

120

CHIGWELL
Oakfields St Winifred's Close
Stanley Keen
1960-61 T A Clark Ltd
A development of flats for sale, good of their period.

CLACTON-ON-SEA

Essex County

Oulton Hall, Marine Parade
A H Devereux
1935
A large guest house with two wings projecting towards the sea and the ground-floor, semi-circular terrace projection between. Rather a bare 1930s otherwise, with banded tower, clock, metal windows and projecting balconies. Clock tower contains the water tanks. Large roof garden. General sea-side stuff. (ABN November 1935.)

Main Concourse   Westwood

Westwood

Snoek

University Sports Pavilion
Barry Gasson and John Meunier
1967
A large brick pavilion with a plan
like the Natwest logo: at the centre
of three rhomboid projections in the
entrance: male and female changing
rooms on either side, and glazed
Bar projecting between. Quite a
discovery.

University of Essex Wivenhoe Park
Architects' Co-Partnership (Kenneth Capon)
1967 Holloway Bros Ltd
One of the group of new Universities established in the
1960s, very much in the public eye, since the
philosophy behind its planning was the subject of the
Reith Lectures in 1963. The site was an eighteenth-
century park (painted by Constable) and the University is tightly planned as a small town straddling the
centre of the valley. All buildings rise from a new
podium below which runs the service road. This tends
to be a series of windswept plazas which singularly fail
to recreate the close-built character of an Italian University hill-town. The architects claim that the building is
designed to provide a community, and anonymous
buildings as a good background to student activities. In
its current state it is much smaller than planned. As
the Vice-Chancellor said: *The place is not finished. You
must imagine it with 10,000 people.* A student population
of that size will only exist in the imagination. Thus it is
a rump University — as is East Anglia; and displays to
a grosser degree than the former the perils of planning
for the unachievable on a large scale.

Architecturally there are traces of ACP's Dunelm
House in Durham (an award winner) all over the place
magnified to a degree. The brick student residence
towers were amongst the first high-rise brickwork buildings in Britain. Another point of interest is the Indoor
Sports Centre, with its mellow red brick and different
coloured string-courses. (Faulkner-Brown, Hendy,
Watkinson, Stonor) 1977 (see J M McKean, *Architect's
Journal*, 20.9.72, for a detailed analysis).

Colchester Youth House
East Stockwell Street
Sir Guy Dawber, Fox & Robinson
1970
A good, plain building with out-
side staircase rising above car park.
Would not survive a Design Guide.

T Street-Porter

Mercury Theatre Balkerne Gardens
Norman Downie & Partners
1972 T J Evers Ltd
Superbly sited base for a repertory company just inside
Colchester's Roman Wall. The ingenious auditorium
planning has the flexibility for both a proscenium with
narrow auditorium, or full auditorium and an open
thrust stage. Glazed first-floor gallery on piloti. However, the rear offices and roof services are much less
skilfully integrated into a unified building form than
the Wolsey Theatre in Ipswich.

McCann

Lion Walk Redevelopment
Frederick Gibberd & Partners in association with
Stanley Bragg and Associates (D Roberts, A Bussell)
1976
A heavy-handed, urban redevelopment in central
Colchester. Odd proportions, overweaning black tiles,
and dark red brick. Plenty commodity, too much
firmness, and light on delight.

Dutch Quarter West Stockwell
Street
Borough Architect's Department
(K Bell, R Rose, R Bishop)
1977
Modern city centre housing, on the
site of a former car park, recreating
the spatial qualities of the old city.
Concrete jettying of upper storeys.

Roachvale County Primary School Roachvale
Essex County Architect's Department (B J Page,
R M B Johnson)
1977
A flat-roofed, system school with concrete panels and
round cornered doors and windows. Good use of colour
but usual problems with projections above the roof.
Splendid light and airy internal spaces, designed to
conserve and recirculate energy. RIBA Commendation. It is fascinating to see Essex County pursue the
system-building and energy conservation theme simul-
taneously with the passive, vernacular. See Thriftwood
School.

DAGENHAM

Architectural Review

Kingswood School Harbourer Road
Yorke Rosenberg Mardall (I Wilson)
1955
Simple two-storey, mid-'50s school,
worth comparing to the contemporary Hertfordshire systems. This
one is much more solid, formal and
architectural: even piloti!

Civic Centre
E Berry Webber
1937
A grand, unlovely Civic Centre by
an architect who designed many
such — including Peterborough.
Traces of Dudok, and modern
architecture — projecting glass bay
windows, brick curves etc. Civic
majesty at its heaviest.

DAGENHAM

Rawles

May and Baker Factory Canteen
Edward D Mills & Partners
1943 Dix Builders Ltd
The first of a number of Mills buildings for May and
Baker was the canteen, completed in 1943, which was
the first architectural use in Britain of a shell concrete
roof. The five arched spans, with glazing beneath,
make this a very elegant and timeless building.
Pharmaceutical Building 1956
Flat, slightly projecting roof, curtain walling on most
sides, save the offices which are brick clad. The main
feature of the factory is the huge central double-height
packing area.

123

DEDHAM

DEDHAM

Erith and Terry

Great House High Street
Raymond Erith
1937-38
This well proportioned, idiosyncratic house is one of Erith's earliest buildings. Very plain, three storeys, pyramid roof — yet underscaled door case, Maverick thermal window immediately above, and shutters on the windows. Said to be 'after Soane'. That cannot be accurate, for Soane would never underscale the centre piece as Erith does so frequently. See Kingswalden Bury (p 165) and Wivenhoe New Park (p 120).

See also houses at **Frog Meadow.** Raymond Erith and Quinlan Terry. 1967-80. Seven houses designed to recapture the essence of a villa-lined street — worth a visit.

EAST HANNING FIELD

DOWNHAM

Plumb

Coulde Dennis Back Lane
James Gowan (G Smith, P Shepheard, P Notley)
1978 T J Evers Ltd
A striking development of terraced houses and blocks of flats in a remote village in Essex. No attempt to be traditional, the flats having patterned brickwork, and the terraces achieving rhythm by a series of mono-pitched and circular chimneys.

House School Lane
Clive Plumb
The pitched roof of this unusual house is supported on free-standing steel columns, with the house space itself arranged beneath and visibly independent of it. A similar construction for the adjoining garage.

FEERING
South Cottage Studios Old Road
Nicholls Associates
1977
Four distinctive court areas linking
studios to study and living facilities.
Derivative of farm buildings, with
black stained panels and diagonal
boarding.

EAST TILBURY

Darley

BATA Workers' Houses
1932
An interesting successor to Silver End, in a group of
houses for this Czech Shoe Company whose great
selling point was design. Modern Movement, spare in
appearance, designed on similar lines to the original
township in Zlin, Czechoslovakia. As far as can be
ascertained, the buildings were designed by engineers,
and have an electrically welded, all-steel frame.

FRINTON PARK Frinton-on-Sea

RIBA

FINGRINGHOE WICK

Essex Naturalists Trust
Headquarters and Interpretive
Centre
Andrew Borges
1976
A pleasant black timber and red
brick pavilion on the edge of the
marshes, with a conning tower for
bird watching.

Oliver Hill (and others)
1934-35
Only a small portion of this grandiose scheme for a
sizeable town, with over a thousand houses, three
churches and a town hall, was ever built. Houses of
different styles were allocated different zones, the most
striking designed by Oliver Hill who was happy to
design buildings in any style. Most interesting is the
circular information kiosk, now converted into a house,
although some of the other houses — which in shape
resemble the Wells Coates house in Welwyn, are worth
a look. Fashionable features include roof terraces, strip
windows, portholes, loggias, balconies and flat roofs,
all within a rather dull suburban layout: seaside architecture derived from ocean-going liners. The proposed
seaside hotel had strong affinities with Hill's Midland
Hotel in Morecambe.

GRAYS

State Cinema George Street
Frank Matcham & Co
1938

According to David Atwell in *Cathedrals of the Movies*, the State is *one of the finest, least altered, and latest in date of the super cinemas.* It retains its original organ. Atwell also draws attention to the Odeon, Brentvogel Street, Bury St Edmunds (George Coles, 1937), Odeon, Lloyds Avenue, Ipswich (George Coles, 1936), Odeon, Dunstable Road, Luton (Andrew Mather, 1938), and the Odeon, Broadway, Peterborough (Harry Weedon, 1937).

Charles

Grays South Redevelopment
Frederick Gibberd & Partners (D Roberts)
1977

Substantial redevelopment of 802 dwellings — flats and three-storey town houses. But for the detail and proportion of the windows, the terraced houses with their projecting party walls provide a pleasant downhill sweep.

GREAT LEIGHS

Plumb

INGATESTONE

Bartram

Own House Castle Close
Clive Plumb
1976

Single-storey, pitched roof, L-shaped house designed by Clive Plumb for his own occupation. Virtually single aspect to the south-west, with solar collector panels on the south front. The architect is a group leader with Basildon Development Corporation Architects responsible for such schemes as Langdon Hills.

Fire Station High Street
Essex County Architect's
Department (J Ferguson)
1976

A one-bay fire station inserted into a small village. Designed with low walls and pitched roof to minimise impact, but its real scale is demonstrated by the heavy handed vehicle access doorway.

HOCKLEY
Forsyte
F E Towndrow
1930

An early modern house of rather heavy and formal appearance, more *Art Deco* than International style. Tall stair tower with oversailing flat roof, the most prominent feature with balconies/sun roofs at both first and second-floor level. The integrated garage gives balance to the plan. The top room trebled as playroom, sun room and dancing room. Towndrow was later to be a joint author of a book on British Cinema Design. The windows have been altered, a garage added and a pergola obtrudes in the purity.

Essex County Council

LOUGHTON

Potter

50 Tycehurst Hill

82 Tycehurst Hill
P D Hepworth
1936

Much more adventurous than the early Cambridge houses, this is a two-storey house with a studio on the third floor. Much play is made of canopies, balconies, loggias and pergolas to give visual excitement to what would otherwise be a plain white box. Set within a fairly formal approach and garden in showing distinct cubist influences. (ABN, September 1936). Hepworth (once a partner of Louis de Soissons) was a prolific house designer of the '20s and '30s, happy to adopt to any style: thatch, half timber, Tudor, Cotswold or Moderne. Note also **50 Tycehurst Hill** (Moderne) (C J Manning Ltd, 1934) and **38 Tycehurst Hill** (P Wynne Williams, 1935).

Potter

HARLOW NEW TOWN

Harlow was one of the first-generation New Towns, designated in 1947 to relieve pressure on London. The site chosen was 37 kilometres north of the east end of London, on the boundary of Essex and Hertfordshire, which then contained 4,500 people. The Development Corporation planned to increase that to 60,000 people, but its success was such that by 1980 the population was 80,000, and its area extended to 6,400 acres. Frederick Gibberd (now Sir) was appointed architect/planner for the New Town: the plan and many of the significant buildings in Harlow are to his design.

The plan is based on four major centres — one being the Town Centre, and the other three neighbourhood centres — Staple Tye, Bush Fair, and The Stow. Old Harlow, to the north-east, was restored, infilled and expanded as a community in its own right and there are smaller centres at Potter Street and Hare Street. Gibberd's influence can be seen in the pattern of patronage of other architects who worked in the town: Maxwell Fry, H T Cadbury Brown, Michael Neylan, Gerard Goalen, Clifford Culpin, Yorke Rosenberg Mardall and Leonard Manasseh.

The two major industrial areas are on the edge of the town — one by the railway and the other to the west. Particular emphasis has been given to landscaping, vehicular segregation and the re-use of older buildings. Natural features such as woodland and streams have been retained and enhanced.

In 1980, after the expenditure of £111.4 million, and the completion of over 24,000 houses, the Development Corporation was wound up and its responsibilities transferred to Harlow District Council. The New Town was new no longer: it had come of age.

Other interesting schemes

Stackhall Housing, Mark Hall North, 1951. Frederick Gibberd.
Housing, Mark Hall North 2A, 1951. Fry Drew and Partners.
Housing, Ladyshot, 1953. Yorke Rosenberg Mardall.
Cooks Spinney Housing, 1952. H T Cadbury Brown.
Brockles Mead Housing, 1972. Leonard Manasseh.

Swift

St Paul's Church
The High Town Centre
Derrick Humphrys
1959
Expressionist brick cruciform church with detached bell tower. Colourful furnishings and mosaic by John Piper.

McCann

Our Lady of Fatima
The Stow
Gerald Goalen
1960
Cruciform, centrally planned church, with a remarkable richness in its windows.

Old Orchard Housing (Competition Winner, Ideal Home). Clifford Culpin and Partners.
Evangelical Lutheran Church, Bush Fair Centre. Robert Maguire and Keith Murray.
St James' Church, Staple Tye, Great Parndon, 1968. Gerard Goalen.
Rivermill Housing, 1965. Frederick Gibberd.
Longbanks Housing, Staple Tye. HDC Design Group.
BP House, Third Avenue, 1967. Wilson, Mason and Partners.
Gilbey's Headquarters, Fourth Avenue, 1964. Peter Falconer.
Advice Centre, Town Centre, 1978. HDC Design Group.

McCann

Market Square The Rows
Frederick Gibberd
1969
Architecture as a flavourless backdrop to colourful activity.

McCann

St James' Church
Great Parndon
Gerard Goalen
1969
Much more restrained than Goalen's Fatima church, looking forward to the Cambridge Chaplaincy Centre (page 36). Has the atmosphere of a pilgrimage chapel.

Gibberd

The Lawn Mark Hall North
Frederick Gibberd (R J Double)
1951
A mixed development of houses, flats, and a tower block in a fine setting of mature trees. The tower is designed on a butterfly plan. It is one of the best examples of contemporary design thought: the terrace houses have pitched roofs and chimneys; the flats have a flat roof and metal windows; and the tower has a three-dimensional quality lost with the later introduction of system-building.

Harlow Civic Centre

Snoek

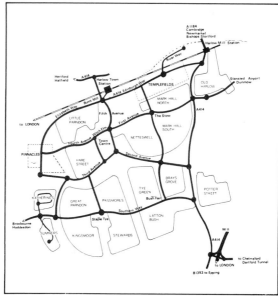

Wainwright

Stackfield Houses Mark Hall North
Frederick Gibberd
1951
Unpretentious, Festival of Britainish terraced houses. Elegant in themselves but failing to create a sense of enclosure. Compare to Roe Green, Hatfield.

McCann

Old Harlow
Frederick Gibberd & Partners
(J Graham)
1970
Old village in the north-east of Harlow has been pedestrianised; gap sites have been filled, and new 'pavilions' erected at the end.

Snoek

Harlow Council

Bishopfield
Michael Neylan
1966
A competition-winning scheme on a sloping site, designed to give the feel of a hillside town: soon nicknamed 'The Casbah' due to its Moorish character. A total, formal contrast to the picturesqueness of much of Harlow's housing. There is an upper-level piazza at the top, enclosed by flats. The sculpture in the photograph is by Gerda Rubenstein. Housing Design Award 1969.

Longman House
Burnt Mill
Frederick Gibberd and Partners
1968
Opposite the railway station, these offices act as an introduction to Harlow and enclose the station forecourt. Elegant rhythm of pre-cast concrete panels.

LOUGHTON

London Transport

London Transport Underground Station
Hall Easton Robertson
1940

A brick box with a great curved, gaping mouth, this station lacks Holden's space-age excitement, but has a certain Scandinavian grandeur about it. It has a notable, cantilevered concrete roof. Note the almost contemporary bus garage by Yorke Rosenberg Mardall.

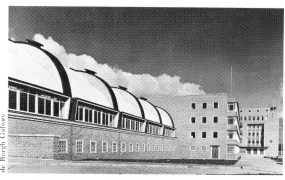

de Burgh Galwey

Special Facilities Building

Westwood

Bank of England Printing Works Langston Road
Easton and Robertson
1954

A significant building spanning the transition between the '30s style (see *Cambridge*, Zoology building) and 'modern architecture'. Some of the old details remain, but they are weak in relation to the overall bulk of the project. Note the use of large-span concrete parabolic arches.

Special Facilities Building for Rank (left)
Precision Industries, Langston Road
Scott, Brownrigg, Turner (N G E Turner, R Martin)
1971

Superb windowless brick box oversailed by its flat roof, whose steel supporting frame provides a form of external steel colonnade. A highly specialised building designed to exacting environmental requirements, it was barely complete before its existing owner was taken over by another which did not require it.

ONGAR

Doctor's Group Surgery Little Bansons, off High Street
John Amor
1976
A simple steel and glass pavilion elevated above a car park in backland Ongar. Two further storeys can be built on top and staff flats beneath, if required in the future. It combines two surgeries, which share waiting areas, reception and staff facilities, but allows for separate practices, nursing staff and records. Not unlike a space capsule, the building has visual affinities with the Thamesmead Health Centre by Derek Stow.

MALDON

Nodrog Farmhouse Moors Farm Chase, Little Totham
Andrew Borges
1976
The cheapest part of the building is usually the roof: this building is all roof. Three A-framed bays are linked together to provide some fine interior spaces.

ROCHFORD

Snoek

Ark House
Yorke Rosenberg Mardall
1964
A neat and precise brick and timber house for the owner of Keddies in Southend (see page 134), arranged at half levels not unlike Laslett house in Cambridge. Double-height living room at the west, over a partially sunken garage/workshop with two floors of other rooms to the east. The facade, with its plain timber cornice, and projecting balconies, is an exercise in elegant visual geometrics.

PURFLEET

Charles

Laboratory Building
Tunnel Portland Cement Co
Sir E Owen Williams
1933
A curtain-walled rectangular structure whose original qualities lay in the simplicity of design, and the cold grey and bright orange paint, which contrasted with surroundings. The original shelving and benching, writing desks were pre-cast concrete with sheet rubber finish on the top.

Darley

Darley

Silver End Village near Braintree
Sir John Burnet & Partners (Thomas Tait)
1926 onwards
A new village built by F H Crittall for workers in his
steel window factory, in Essex farmland. Before the
Depression struck, over 500 houses had been built,
some detached and some in terraces. Crittall wrote: *In
planning the houses we decided to sacrifice traditional design in
the cause of air and light and space.* The architects were
Thomas Tait of Sir John Burnet & Partners (soon to
be Sir John Burnet, Tait & Lorne), C H B Quennell,
and C M Hennell. The most interesting buildings are
those by Tait, which, in 1926, were very much ahead
of their time in Britain. The most imposing buildings
are 'Le Chateau' and the Estate Manager's house
(designed by Frederick McManus and under Tait's
direction). Tait was clearly influenced by the Behrens
house in Northampton, and it shows particularly in the
Estate Manager's house. Flat roof, oversailing
balconies, hoods and porches, triangulated glass
windows, metal strip windows, and plain white-washed
brickwork.

133

Snoek

Keddies Store Warrior Square
Yorke Rosenberg Mardall
1963
This extension to an existing department store comprises three-storey shop, and parking, surmounted by
eight floors of offices. The podium is rather blank with
thin strip windows running the length of the building
between white glazed tiles. The design of the office
storey above has the soulless precision to be expected
from these architects. Despite that, more quality than
Southend had reason to expect. Civic Trust Award
1964.

Central Library Victoria Avenue
Southend Borough Architect's Department
(R P Bleksley, A C Membery, A Wornell)
1974
The architects were asked to design a popular library
within the Civic Centre. The result is a series of
libraries arranged round a central core, the lower
storeys clothed in glass, the upper storeys in concrete
held up by columns. A smart, neat job. Some distant
echoes of Lasdun's Royal College of Physicians.

SOUTH WOODHAM FERRERS

Ten miles from Chelmsford, Essex County Council, together with private developers, are grafting a small country town upon existing villages, plotlands and scrublands. The aim is to concentrate new demand into a town so as to stem the sporadic rash of new estates. Target population is 17,500 (a four-fold expansion), with completion by the late 1980s. The majority of development will be residential, but there will be two industrial areas and the town centre. The town is the apotheosis of the 'Design Guide for Residential Areas'. Design briefs are prepared for each area. Already, some of the results can be seen. The town centre (Holder and Mathias) pillages the past for visual references — occasionally wittily. The sense of enclosure is right, but the feeling is ersatz. Some towns hire a town artist: South Woodham Ferrers needs to hire its Long John Silver, Ben Gunn and Robinson Crusoe.

Primary School
Essex County Council Architects

Advance Industrial Units

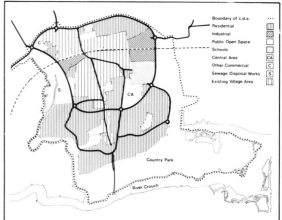

Town Centre

Fenn Farm Houses
Stanley Keen & Partners
(E R Bryan)
1977
A pilot scheme designed to demonstrate the principles of the *Essex Design Guide.* Eighteen houses planned in a variety of different settings — such as main road, mews court, private drives.

135

Flats Church Road
N Martin-Kaye
1931
Two-storey block, balcony, cut away
corners rather neat plan, relatively
spacious internally: covered in ice-
cream render, and sadly lacking the
original timber pergola.

Hassenbrook School
Gerald Lacoste and Partners (K Dod, C Ross)
1952
Immediate post-war school worth comparing to the
system-schools which had overrun Hertfordshire. Very
'30-ish, with Swedish tower, long, low, horizontals and
spectacular brickwork — particularly around the
doorway.

WESTCLIFF

White Walls Clatterfield Gardens
N Martin-Kay
1934
Small private house adjacent to the White Hall
community building, also by Martin-Kaye. Usual, two-
storey flat-roofed building distinguished by triangulated
window ex. Silver End. White rendered and well maintained. Stylish for its area.

WITHAM

Maltby

Cooper Taber Seed Warehouse
Chamberlin Powell & Bon (F R Holroyd,
J Connaughton)
1955
Two separate buildings — the Processing Building
which is a vertically designed cubic steel cage, sitting
on a blue brick plinth, containing processing equipment etc; and the Warehouse which is a horizontally
designed building lower in height. The clarity with
which the various parts of the building are put together
is a delight, as is the way contrasts between black and
white, are achieved, and the boxing out of the escape
staircase from the Warehouse. There is a faint
Japanese air to the latter. From the architects' point of
view, the job was *lovely engineering, and the client just
wrote four letters.* Visible from the railway.

WRITTLE

10 Chancery Place The Green
David Brewster
1969
A house, hand built by the architect with the aim of
obtaining the largest usuable volume. Most of the
space is on the ground floor, but the pitched roof
construction has allowed the provision of a gallery in
the roof.

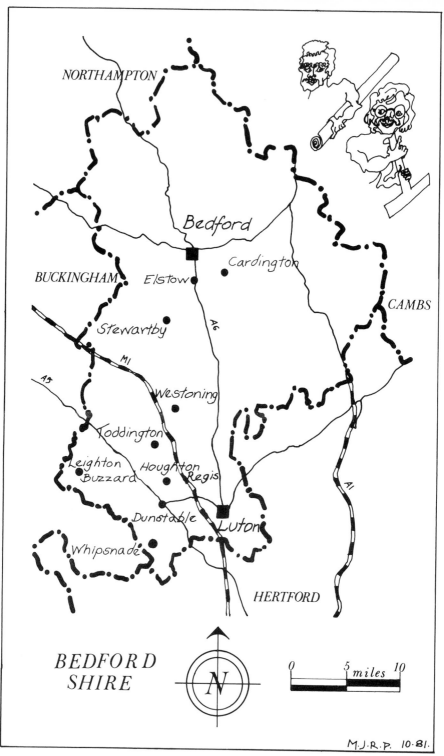

NORTHAMPTON

Bedford

Cardington

BUCKINGHAM

Elstow

CAMBS

A6

Stewartby

M1

A5

Westoning

Toddington

Leighton
Buzzard

Houghton
Regis

Dunstable

Luton

A1

Whipsnade

HERTFORD

BEDFORD
SHIRE

N

0   5 miles 10

M.J.R.P. 10.81.

138

BEDFORDSHIRE

Bedfordshire is a county largely by-passed by great surviving monuments or glorious towns and cities: largely by-passed by history as well. Although Bedford is the county town, that former centre of hat-making, Luton, is undoubtedly the heart of the county. It is not a town that has much surviving townscape or historic character; but it does have a number of individual buildings of interest. Bedford is an ancient market town (home of John Bunyan) overtaken by Victorian sprawl, and very nearly destroyed by modern developments and traffic systems.

The County as a whole has two or three main modern calls on glory: first, the great airship sheds at Cardington; second, bricks and brick stacks and the attached village of Stewartby; and finally the glories of Whipsnade Zoo, providing this book with the only examples of the outstanding work of the 1930s firm of Berthold Lubetkin and Tecton (and also the only pink flamingoes, white rhinoceri, etc).

BEDFORD

Bedfordshire County Council

Dame Alice Harpur School
Oswald P Milne
1938

Chunky brick neo-Dutch school. One of a number of contemporary Milne educational buildings in this area. The Architecture Club selected it as one of the buildings to illustrate their book on inter-war architecture in 1940. Milne also designed the Science Block at Bedford School in 1933, and worked at nearby Stewartby.

Mander Technical College Cauldwell Street
Bedfordshire County Architects (J H Bramwell,
A W Johns, H Hartley, A Chrystal, M J Long)
1958
Eight-storey teaching block with kitchen and refectory
on the banks of the Great Ouse. It is a fascinating
historical case study. It was severely criticised by the
Architect's Journal of the time (*mirable dictu*) for being too
concerned with external appearance and unnecessary
elaboration. Great play was made of the decision to
stretch the communal rooms on the ground floor to two
floors to achieve greater height. Looking at it now, it is
amazing to think of this building as being *too* decorative. What is clear is that the individual details which
caused so much controversy did not in themselves do
anything to change the overall nature of this squat
block: and therein lies much of the history of the '50s.

Christ Church Goldington Road
N F Cachemaille-Day
1956-58
Cachemaille-Day was a notable
church architect and co-operated
with architects Welch and Lander
on Park Royal Underground Station
and other schemes.

Texas Instruments Menton Lane
O'Neil Ford & Colley
Facory with a series of hyperbolic
paraboloid concrete shell roofs.

North Beds BC

Bedford Library Harpur Street
Bedford Borough Architect (E B Heath)
1972
An interesting development whereby the ground floor
is mostly let to the shop next door, with the library,
coffee shop etc being above it. The visual spoor of
Lasdun's Royal College of Physicians quite clear in the
top storey. The whole building is sophisticated, but
rather too monumental both for Bedford and for this
particular street.

Bedfordshire County Council

Drama Hall Bedford College of
Higher Education, Lansdowne Road
**Bedford County Architect's
Department** (T Wall)
1966
Really a multi-purpose building
including music and practice rooms,
this triangular, brick building is
primarily used for teaching dancing.

Verby

Graylaw House Goldington Road
Peter Smith & Partners (R A Lee)
1972
A small, orange brick block of offices, currently occupied by VAT Inspectorate. A neat addition to a drab street. Eastern Region Certificate of Merit, 1973.

Alleway

County Hall and Library
Bedfordshire County Architect's Department
(D J Chalk, I C Hill)
1969 Arthur Sanders Ltd
This civic castle is a formal, quasi-Brutalist conception across the river from the main town. The development consists of three contiguous buildings arranged on a landscaped plinth, around a 'water feature'. The architectural approach is hard, horizontal and concrete with certain Cubist interplays on the library facade. It leaves the probably inaccurate impression of a cold, aloof and remote council; ironic in view of nearby Northampton's rejection of their competition-winning glass pyramid office, on just those grounds. The curve of the main administration block together with its open parapet lifts the building out of the ordinary.

North Beds BC

Harpur Shopping Centre
Harpur Street
Frederick Gibberd & Partners
(M Davies)
1978 Keir Construction Ltd
The adaptation of the former Bedford Modern School (Blore, 1829-30 stone, neo-Tudor) into a modern shopping centre, with a completely new building behind: the use of the old building is interesting, but the exterior of the new development is undistinguished.

Donat

Bedford Midland Station
BR London Midland Region (J Sanders)
1978
A replacement of a fine Victorian station with British Rail's modern. Obviously more compact, and, for the time being, very much brighter and more glittering. Plentiful use of glass and steelwork and all the high-tech paraphenalia. It is a scaled-up version of the anaesthetic and colourful little boxes British Rail have introduced into London suburbia.

CARDINGTON

R100 and R101 at Cardington

Airship Hangars
No. 1 (left-hand) 1916-17, enlarged in the mid-1920s to the present dimensions of 812 feet long, 180 feet clear width, and 156 feet high. No. 2 (right-hand). Brought from Norfolk and re-erected at Cardington in 1922. A Gargantuan exercise in pre-fabrication, using the girder techniques employed in the construction of actual airships. The hangars dominate the countryside for many miles with a brooding grace: they are currently used for the Fire Research Establishment. The photograph shows them with the R100 and R101 airships still in their metal nests (right).

DUNSTABLE

Gliding Club interior as finished

London Gliding Club, off Tring Road
Christopher Nicolson
1934-35
An altered building, with some affinities to Mendelsohn's Bexhill Pavilion: long, low body, with prominent semi-circular glazed projection. An appropriately stream-lined image for aeroplanes. Yet with its brick tower and attached clock, it is an odd fusion between the International style and the Dutch brick influence.

RIBA

Dunstable Fire Station
County Architect's Department
1962-65
Found favour with Pevsner.

Potter

Windsock Public House West Road
Smith & Wilson-Smith
1965

A magnificent 'character' pub, echoing the air-shapes of the nearby Gliding Club. Sadly, the idea is not thorough enough to make the building much more than a thoroughly shocking vulgarity, or a thoroughly enjoyable shock. The photograph tells no lies: the floors are really canted. An excellent building for stimulating an architect's adrenalin, and well worth a detour.

HOUGHTON REGIS

GLC

ELSTOW

Cottages Bunyan's Mead
Chrystal & West
1979

The restoration of splendid mediaeval and seventeenth-century buildings, with new houses for North Bedfordshire District Council in the long, narrow, mediaeval gardens behind. Steep pitch roofs, boarding and second-hand pantiles. More a question of the right atmosphere than innovative architecture.

Parkside Housing Development
GLC Town Development Division (J Lawler)
1978

A very successful example of instant tradition, with excellent planting, a warm reddish brick and good tiling. Although fine in small chunks, the style could become oppressive, were it too widely adopted. The fashionable pantiled mono-pitched roof is evident. The layout is designed so that the central areas are car-free and safe for children. It is the last of four schemes built by the GLC in South Bedfordshire, and has 564 flats, patio houses and large family houses.

LEIGHTON BUZZARD

Kyle

Gladley House
Peter Dunham (Charter Building Design)
1971
A very clever house for the architect's own occupation. Single-storey brick and timber, yet using the fall in the site to achieve differing volumes, clerestorey lighting, and a remarkably expressive exposed timber roof. Part of the house is cantilevered but over the hillside. In plan the house consists of two neatly intersecting rectangles at different levels.

LUTON

St Andrew's Church Blenheim Crescent
Sir Giles Gilbert Scott
1931-32
A massive, buttressed, brick building, which impresses by its sheer grandeur inside as outside: a Valhalla for brick layers. Austere interior, with clever lighting effects. Luton has a number of other interesting churches within the period, including: **All Saints,** Shaftesbury Road (1922-23), by W D Caroë. Caroë was a noted church architect, particularly for his work in Wales. **St Christopher,** Round Green, (1936-37) by Sir Albert Richardson. Richardson continued to refine Georgian architecture when others were going modern. Pevsner called this church, *very reactionary.* Also **St Francis,** Carteret Road, 1959-60, by P Dunham, Widdup & Harrison (later founding partners of Charter Building Design Group); and finally **St Luke,** Oakley Road, Leagrave (1956) by Lord Mottistone (Seely & Paget).

LUTON
Vauxhall Motor Co Offices
Kimpton Road
H B Cresswell
1907-15
Properly speaking, outside our period, but Cresswell became famous for being the author of the *Honeywood File.* Interesting to see what he himself designed: traditional, William and Mary brick building.

Midland Road Railway Station
W H Hamlyn (Chief Architect, London-Midland-Scottish Railway Co)
1938-40
Designed in the mud-brown brick style that buildings influenced by Dutch Modernism took: however, if it had any sparkle then, it has surely lost it now: the glazed bridge is new, and additions have spoilt its original lines. The original impact is best judged from the entrance, where the chunky, geometric massing can still be appreciated.

LUTON *(continued)*

Municipal Buildings George Street
Bradshaw, Gass & Hope
1936
Winner of a competition held in 1930, this is a grand, unappealing neo-classical design, pared to its basic essentials and capped by a squat tower over a giant portico. Entrance hall reasonably stylish: the remainder traditional. The architects, like Cowles-Voysey, Berry Webber and James and Pierce, seemed to specialise in Town Halls.

Boys' Secondary School
(now Sixth Form College), Badgers Hill Road
Marshall & Tweedy
1938
Very well worth seeing for British compromise between European modern architecture and native traditions, this building comprises a main block with double wings, linked to an arts and crafts wing, and a number of classrooms. Its principal interest lies in the combination of curve and square: the main curving staircase is spectacular; and the headmaster's office and a first-floor greenhouse project in semi-circular fashion. The scheme was a competition prizewinner designed by Hungarian refugee, Turok, formerly of the Vienna State Architect's Department.

BUILDING THE FUTURE ON FIRM FOUNDATIONS

The award winning extension to the 12th century Parish Church of St. Mary at Luton.

For over a century, T.E. Neville Ltd. have worked hand in hand with a variety of clients.

A firm commitment, whether in Contracting, Building Services, Joinery or Team Design Construction, will enable us to remain a strong `Teamforce´ within every area of the future building industry.

T & E NEVILLE LIMITED
MARSH ROAD, LEAGRAVE,
LUTON LU3 2RZ

For further information please contact:
Peter Henman or Chris Worrell on (0582) 53456

Lambert

Airport Terminal
Yorke, Rosenberg Mardall
1966
A single-storey, flat-roofed building, with canted eaves
and rhythm of steel columns. Very neat and simple:
but could have been more. Note also *Hangar* (1970)
also by Y R M.

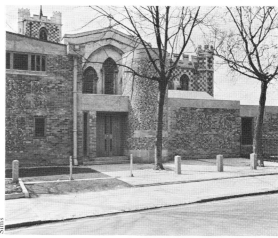

Sims

Police Station Buxtable Road
Bedfordshire County Architect's
Department
1976 C Miskin & Sons
Crisply detailed but harsh building
in fashionable red engineering brick.
An altogether forbidding develop-
ment.

Caledonian House
Hastings Street/Stuart Street
M W T Architects (G B Woods
and R H White)
1976 J M Hill & Sons
Oddly scaled red brick offices facing
the bypass, distinctive for their
projecting stair towers.

St Mary's Church Hall
George G Pace
1969 Neville Construction Ltd
St Mary's is Luton's finest church, predominantly
fifteenth century, and constructed of flint and stone
chequer work. The extension, which includes the
church hall and ancillary offices, has been designed to
match the materials, albeit in a modern style. Once
again, flint and stone is used, but in a modern (post-
and-beam) rather than Gothic form. The workmanship
is excellent, and the impact on the original church one
of improvement rather than otherwise.

Whiting

Luton Industrial Mission
Charter Building Design Group (A Hucklesby)
1976
Seven-storey residential tower with pre-cast concrete arcading up to the entrance. The development also includes a chapel, refectory and lecture theatres. The Mission provides courses in industrial relations jointly for management and unions.

Reid

Flats Stoneways Close, Toddington Road
Farrell Grimshaw Partnership (D Clark, R Bryant, J Foges, J Chatwin, J Cole)
1977 Kerridge (Cambridge) Ltd
One of three similar schemes in Luton designed by the Farrell Grimshaw Partnership for the Maunsel Housing Association. Unusual timber-framed construction of the upper storeys, resting on the solid ground storeys. In some cases this division is one between a ground-storey flat and an upper maisonette. There is good use of colour for such items as window frames, and clever planning. Otherwise, the building's appearance is rather blank, relying on the occasional balcony or timber staircase detail for any interest. See also Dunstable Road and Crawley Green Road, all in Luton. They are all of primarily the same constructional interest.

Luton Borough Council

Kahn Factory
P E Williams (Staff Architect to Richard Ellis)
1969
A strangely formal street facade for a factory, between two bright red brick towers. It does not quite come off, but was worth a shot at trying formality instead of technology for this type of building.

148

TODDINGTON

Bedfordshire County Council

Library Market Square
County Architect's Department
(T Wall, C J Lathwell)
1972 Icknield Builders Ltd
A red brick library with a fine dormer-lit gallery for the reference collection. There is contrast but no tension between the irregularity of the facade below the eaves, and the regimentation of the dormer windows above.

Kyle

Two Waters Park Road
Keith Miller
1973
One of a pair of steel and glass houses cantilevered from a hillside in Toddington, both designed for architects. The Miller house has unusually clean lines and modernity for Bedfordshire, although it lacks the sparkle of its contemporary equivalents in Hampstead. The use of the slope solves car-parking and view at a stroke.

150

STEWARTBY

This estate village was constructed by the London Brick Company, and is dominated by the brick kiln chimneys. The character is generally speaking brick neo-colonial, or neo-Georgian, and the architects were as follows: the village hall, by **Vincent Harris** (1928-30); the club, also by Harris (1928-30); the Secondary Modern School by **Oswald P Milne** (1936-37); and the Old People's Homes by **Richardson and Houfe** (1955-56).

WESTONING

Log cabin interior

MacIntyre Schools Westoning Manor
MacCormac & Jamieson
1976 Grange Construction
The only major work by these architects in Eastern England is a group of log cabins hidden on landscaped slope in part of the mature grounds of an old manor house. The development provides residential houses for mentally handicapped children, and the structure chosen is a Swedish log-cabin system, which was specifically selected for its therapeutic effect on the children. Wide, overhanging eaves and low-pitched roofs, combine with the buildings being well set into the sloping site, to give the group their rustic flavour. Each house is designed with wings of bedrooms and lavatories radiating from a central, top-lit communal area.

Zoological Society of London: M Lyster

Elephant House Whipsnade Zoo
Lubetkin and Tecton
1934-35
A building which *Architect and Building News* claimed
made architectural history. Fresh from working at the
London Zoo, on the Gorilla House and Penguin Pool
where (it was recorded) the breeding season broke all
records, Tecton designed this long, low building for
four elephants, bounded by an eight-foot-deep pool.
There is a circular, top-lit pavilion for each elephant.
The original glass has been replaced with fibre glass.
The architect's stated aim was to *achieve the health and
happiness of the animals.* Note the contemporary *Giraffe
House.*

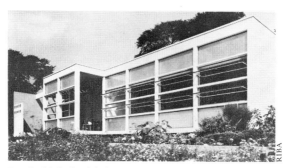

RIBA

Berthold Lubetkin's country cottage
Lubetkin and Tecton
1936
On a most enviable site on the edge of the Chilterns,
one of two houses was for the zoo, and the other for
Berthold Lubetkin himself: the latter has the greater
interest. Its exterior and interior are planned as a unit,
with curving screen walls, loggias and a roof terrace.
The interior plan is free flowing. Glass bricks surround
the front door, and there is constant pleasure in the
contrast between rectangle and curve. The plan,
having many similarities to Highpoint, is a delight.
Arguably, the house is one of the finest architectural
creations of the '30s in Britain.

Lubetkin's country cottage

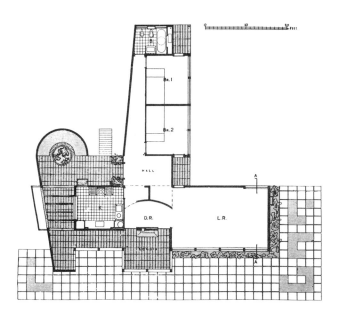

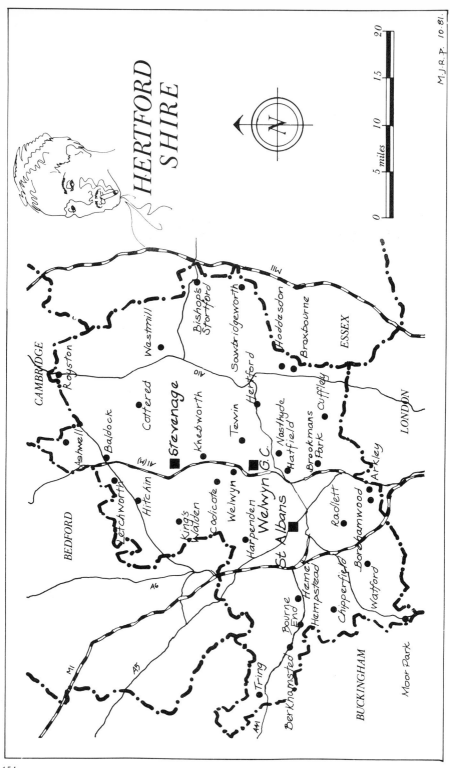

HERTFORDSHIRE

HERTFORDSHIRE

As a county, Hertfordshire must have one of the most representative selection of post-1920 architecture of anywhere in Britain. The reasons for that may be several: first, its proximity to London, as the home of the more affluent and trendy commuters who felt that Essex was somewhat downmarket. Perhaps a more important reason is the presence in the county of the first two Garden Cities, Letchworth and Welwyn, whose presence generated a willingness to experiment.

In 1920, Letchworth was still in an Arts and Crafts phase, but by now somewhat fading. The new pioneer was Welwyn Garden City whose development attracted — in addition to the standard neo-Georgian of the time — houses by Wells Coates (1935), a factory by Soissons and Kenyon (1926) and the Roche building by Otto Salvisberg (1939). The finest road house of the period, the Comet (1933) is to be found in Hatfield in a style not dissimilar to that of the Addis factory in Hertford (1935). Welwyn provided the home for an interesting house by refugee E C Kaufman (1937-38) and a handsome, almost British, modern house next door by Paul Mauger (1937). These, however, are not the famous ones. Connell Ward and Lucas left one of their less exciting products at Moor Park (1936), F R S Yorke chose Nast Hyde for his most unusual creation, Torilla (1935), and it was at Chipperfield Common that Maxwell Fry battled for his flat-roofed, concrete artist's house — partially unsuccessfully (1935). Mary Crowley's development of four houses at Tewin (1936) anticipated the post-war Festival of Britain style with startling clarity.

The most significant post-war development was the declaration of the New Towns in 1946 — particularly Welwyn/Hatfield and Stevenage. The former has become an example of all those very British attempts to match pretty British cottages with post-war building austerity and aesthetic barrenness. Buildings by Brett and Boyd (Lord Esher) and Tayler and Green in Roe Green are worth a visit for historic reasons. The fact that the new Hatfield failed to create the same sense of architectural enclosure as the old is to be regretted: but it was the fashion of the time. Stevenage, by contrast, has matured with its later housing schemes, some of which still remain examples of the glorious '60s: privacy, fine planting, and simple and unostentatious houses. Its road segregation policy was pioneering and some of its factories were very fine. Sadly, its centre — with its slender clock-tower — has failed to live up to the complexity required of town centres.

The County Architect's Department, under C H Aslin, made a name for itself in the immediate post-war years, in developing a system of lightweight panel prefabricated schools, the earliest examples of which were so neatly disposed in fine landscaped settings that they had the air of pavilions in the park.

ASHWELL
Ashwell Bury

An early nineteenth-century house extensively re-modelled by **Sir Edwin Lutyens (1922-26)**. He rendered the main elevation to the building, added a new doorcase, and affected a great improvement in the fenestration by the addition of shutters. Typical Lutyens details such as cornices, red brick chimney stacks, and a staircase which recedes in its upper storey.

BALDOCK

Flats North Road
Priestman Bennett & Partners (A Woollerson)
1979

A sensitively scaled and pleasantly coloured scheme of flats in separate two-storey blocks on the outskirts of Baldock. Worth a second if not third look, despite rather heavy dormer windows.

BISHOPS STORTFORD

Railway Station
BR Eastern Region Architect's Dept (R Fawcett)
1962

A skilful part-restoration, and part new railway station: a bright spaceframe in the ticket office, and the brick drum contains the station master's office. See also the Mainstream Station at Broxbourne (1960) and the '70s version at Stevenage.

ARKLEY
House Alyn Close
off Barnet Lane
John Voelcker
1959

One of the few buildings completed by this architect, one of the original members of Team Ten. Built for Humphrey Lyttleton.

BERKHAMSTED
Offices and Shops
High Street
Melvin Lansley & Mark
1976

Fairly pleasant red brick infill scheme, nicest for Boots, dominated by a higher office block behind. Plenty of lead.

St Paul's School
Gollins Melvin Ward Partnership
1977

A real aberration: a circular plan village school by one of Britain's best commercial practices celebrated for their neo-Miesian Commercial Union development in London. A rather peculiar domed result and foreshortened facade.

BISHOPS STORTFORD

Memorial Hall
Bishops Stortford College
Clough Williams Ellis
1921-22

A rather grand neo-classical building, complete with urns on the corners. This building has an elegance which many neo-Georgian buildings of the '20s failed to achieve. (Drawing by Mrs Shiela Pittuck.)

156

BOREHAMWOOD
Factory, A1 (Barnet bypass)
Wallis Gilbert & Partners
1938
Although much altered, this factory is the only one in Eastern England by Wallis, Gilbert and Partners who were responsible for a fine series of inter-war factories (including the Hoover factory in Perivale, West London). This brick job is not up to their usual style: the entrance is at a corner capped by a tower, with two wings enclosing a rectangular factory behind. Perhaps its dullness is because it was speculative, or because it was a late job. Note the former RNLI building alongside, with canopy and projecting semi-circular tower.

Offices for District Council and Charringtons
T F P Architects with Abbot Howard
(A G Kimberley)
1973 J A Elliott Ltd
A very metropolitan development in a county market town of offices for the District Council and offices for Charringtons. Very smooth round curtain walling on a red brick plinth. Although elegant, the overall impact is too heavily metropolitan for this location.

BOREHAMWOOD

Research Laboratories Elstree Way
Austin-Smith, Lord
1972 J Willmott Holdings Ltd
Interesting and sleek laboratories for Hunting Survey Consultants. Also includes computer suite and administration. Nice contrast between horizontality of building and the rolling landscape.

BROXBOURNE

BROXBOURNE

Lambert

Railway Station
BR Eastern Region (T Rainier)
1962

Lido
Lee Valley Regional Park Architects (J M Bishop,
J M Jarns, M G Quinton)
1978

A glass enclosed £4.2 million leisure complex, mostly swimming pool with wave-making machine. Bright colours and sophisticated detailing and planning make it attractive in what was a semi-derelict area: yet both the building and the pool seem somewhat shallow.

BOURNE END
Watermill Hotel
Melvin Lansley & Mark
1973

A sensitive restoration/rebuilding of a nineteenth-century corn-grinding mill, with a wing of bedrooms to one side. Awful interiors (not the architects') and peculiar off-pitch pyramid roofs.

CHIPPERFIELD

Little Winch, The Common

Little Winch as completed

BROOKMAN'S PARK
BBC London Regional Wireless Station Great North Road
Guthrie Wimperis Simpson
1929
A heavy, static building in stone, constructed as the first of a series to extend broadcasts throughout Britain. Interesting principally for historical reasons.

Little Winch, The Common
E Maxwell Fry
1935
An artist's house in stockbroker land which encountered grave problems in getting planning permission, succeeding only at the fourth try, and substantially modified. The Council's discussions were arcane: the virtues of a flat roof versus a pitched roof, and the vexed problem of materials. *Mr Fry said that the building would be of reinforced concrete which allowed them to make full use of the cheap electricity they provided in Watford, and also allowed big windows. The Chairman said the main thing was whether the council wanted, a concrete house in Chipperfield Common.* Fry won the roof but lost the concrete. The house is built of local stock brick and weatherboarding. The garden front now is barely visible behind creeper, which is its saving grace. Architecturally the house is very similar to Fry's competition entry for a concrete house: large sliding picture windows for the living room, strip windows upstairs and an external staircase. In formal terms, it is little more than a utilitarian cladding on a spacious and elegant interior.

CODICOTE

Miller

The Node Dairy
Maurice Chesterton
1927-29
Built for a wealthy and eccentric American businessman, the dairy set new standards for hygenic and efficient dairy farming in England. It is also something of a romantic folly. It is designed around a circular central courtyard with outward curving wings. The silo storage is raised to form a dramatic tower. The whole complex is thatched — even a conveyor for dung on its way to the heap.

COTTERED

Lambert

Cottered Primary School
Melvin Lansley & Mark
1976
A small primary school in a remote village positively displaying the virtues of invisibility. To be found at the end of a long, white wall, its most prominent feature is the huge orange pantiled roof.

Garden House
Charter Building Design Group
1976
A simple timber-framed house raised above a basement, overlooking one of the two authentic classical Japanese gardens in Britain, created 70 years ago by Herbert Goode. The house has a pleasant neo-American Colonial atmosphere about it: ideal for Mint Juleps on the balcony to the strumming of banjos.

CUFFLEY

St Andrew's Church Plough Hill
Clifford Culpin & Partners
1965
A-frame structure (again) on a commanding site, with entirely glazed gable. Its simple elegance is somewhat distorted by the concrete ramps and walkways that lead across its facade, and up to the main entrance. Would have been greatly enhanced by a simple flight of steps instead.

HARPENDEN

Snock

Ferrum House Grange Court Road
John S Bonnington
1963
A most elegant house, classically planned with a steel piano-nobile surmounting a smaller brick podium which contains the entrance, laundry etc. The steel box (which effectively contains the house) seems perched on its brick walls which themselves enclose — in an almost eighteenth-century formal manner — a garden. Detailing is precise and cool. The house has been extended beyond the garden wall since it was first built.

HATFIELD

Potter

The Comet Hatfield Bypass
E B Musman
1933
The most streamlined example of the peculiar British brick version of modernism, in the form of a pub on the Hatfield bypass. The whole of the bypass is lined with buildings redolent of the great days of the Great North Road. The Comet's use of banded brick and glass with curved projections on all sides is extremely stylish. Its plan is the outline of an aeroplane. A very superior road house, although less so now than it has been. Musman was also responsible for the Nag's Head in Dunmow Road, Bishops Stortford (1936).

Potter

Hatfield Polytechnic
Easton & Robertson
1951-53 Gilbert Ash Ltd
Hertfordshire County Council
(Project Architect: R Moye)
1977 T A Bickerton & Son Ltd
Begun in 1951 on a huge site beside the Barnet bypass, the original buildings were designed by Easton and Robertson, in a style clearly recognisable as being of its time — with a full-height glazed gable, boxed out windows and slender porch canopies. Equally typically, it has a sculpture by Barbara Hepworth, by Reg Butler, a painting by Ben Nicholson, and relief by Trevor Tennant. Of the later buildings, one of the most interesting, by virtue of its complete contrast with the original buildings, is the students' communal building nicknamed by them *The Elephant House.* This is virtually a Students' Union, with a shop, bank, refreshment lounge area, and recreation rooms on the lower level.

Lamber

The Ryde
Peter Phippen Associates
1966

HATFIELD

Swimming Pool Cavendish Way
Woodroffe Buchanan & Coulter
1966
One of the largest hyperbolic paraboloid lightweight concrete shell roofs in Europe.

Roe Green Neighbourhood
Lionel Brett and
Kenneth Boyd
1952
A large development of houses and flats largely devoid of the stylistic traces of the Festival of Britain. The two-storey terraced houses are usually slightly staggered, offset one from the next, which permits ingenious planning but does not create an urban streetscape. Reddish brick, pitched roofs, dinky chimneys and serried ranks of downwater pipes.

Redhall Lane Housing
Welwyn Hatfield District Council
Architect's Department
(G Waterhouse)
1978 Walker & Titmus
Interesting attempt to create a new image for rural council housing. Designed like a series of large-roofed barns.

The Ryde

This is a pioneering housing scheme in many senses: one of the first co-ownership schemes in the country with a full Council mortgage and bridging loan; a new attempt at providing good houses cheaply but with high-quality architectural design; and finally a development of the courtyard form of house. These are terraced houses, single storey in height which let sunlight and fresh air into every room by means of courtyards throughout their length. In good weather the various rooms facing onto the courtyard can open out into the courtyard themselves. Although the houses are now semi-invisible behind abundant greenery, their original aesthetic was determined by concrete blockwork and black stained horizontal timber fascias.

HEMEL HEMPSTEAD
Town Hall
Clifford Culpin & Partners
1965
A rather bland version of the corporate design of the early 1960s, arranged around an internal courtyard ' with the Council Chamber at the centre. Few positive architectural virtues. Now subject to a competition winning extension by Melvin Lansley & Mark, currently shelved.

Kodak House
T P Bennett & Son
1971
Kodak's Headquarters facing a traffic roundabout in Hemel Hempstead: gigantic in its setting, yet with certain elegance of scale.

Grove Hill Centre Henry Wells Square
Melvin Lansley & Mark (D Brooke)
1977 Joseph Driver Ltd
Like two large white boats stranded in a depressing housing estate on the outskirts of Hemel Hempstead, the new centre consists of linked pavilions with expressionist aluminium roofs. The building complex includes a multi-denominational church, a chapel, cafe and a dance hall, catering facilities, club room and bar. The almost orange colour of the wood, contrasts with the gleaming white exterior to make this new building the community landmark a church should be: in colour and form, if not in height.

HEMEL HEMPSTEAD

Hunt

Computer Technology Building
Eaton Road
Foster Associates
1969
An early long-life, loose-fit building.

163

Potter

Addis Factory Ware Road
Douglas Hamilton
1935 Extended 1955
This toothbrush factory is one of the few good
examples of early industrial architecture in Eastern
England. Yet it differs substantially from the rendered
jazz extravagances of Wallis Gilbert. Instead, it chooses
the currently fashionable style for education buildings
(Cray Valley Technical School, Sidcup etc); low brick
and glass wing with substantial curved, full glazed,
staircase towers. The portholes, white-rendered walls, and
ocean liner paraphenalia came later. Perhaps there are
echoes of Mendelssohn's Schocken stores in Stuttgart,
but here in Hertford the proportions are more lumpy.

County Hall and Extension Pegs Lane
James & Bywaters and Roland Pierce
1939 C Miskin & Son
Hertfordshire County Architect's Department (P Wakely)
1971-76
The original building was a competition winner, a mixture
of neo-Georgian and Scandinavian. Altogether relatively
uninspiring from the outside. Extended by the County
Architect's Department with blocks of administrative offices,
and lower linking blocks to the original building providing
space for members' facilities.

Hitchin Library

HITCHIN
Public Library
Martin Priestman Architects
1964
An inspiring extension to a Victorian building in
central Hitchin, whose black and white cantilevered
upper storey, projecting walls and pergolas, conveys an
image of sleek modernity, also carried through inside.

Eurich.

HODDESDON
Rye House Power Station
Essex Road
Sir Giles Gilbert Scott
1954
A post-war power station by Sir Giles Gilbert Scott, grandson of Battersea Power Station (1935): some similarities, but not so convincing.

Merck Sharpe and Dohme Factory
Edward Mills & Partners
1968
Production building and offices, of greater architectural interest than normal: two-storey, steel-framed block on top of concrete and brick podium, and capped by recessed glazed office accommodation.

Lambert

Civic Hall
Hutchison Locke and Monk (T W Goulbourn)
1976
A large, multi-purpose hall, with a small hall, kitchen, services, bar, meeting room etc, set well into a hillside above a lake. The bulk of the hall dominates the entire complex, designed almost warehouse-fashion with red brick, seemingly windowless buttressed projections. Windows are concealed from view in the buttress reveals.

KINGS WALDEN

Kings Walden Bury
Raymond Erith & Quinlan Terry
1972
Replacing a burnt-out, neo-Elizabethan house, this Venetian mansion is perhaps the apotheosis of Erith and Terry's work. All the quirks are here: the use of the Venetian foot in scale, the plain, projecting wings, the recessed centrepiece, round-headed windows and loggias. The north front demonstrates the peculiarity of the major pedimented feature being lower and less significant than its adjoining wings. (See *Dedham*, Essex.) The garden facade is particularly fine and has echoes of Williamsburg.

LETCHWORTH GARDEN CITY TRAIL

The Master Plan for Letchworth by Barry Parker and Raymond Unwin, adopted as a result of a limited competition early in 1904, set environmental standards which directly influenced local authority housing and ultimately state-developed New Towns. Raymond Unwin spent several months examining site characteristics prior to drawing up his initial plan. The plan contained important land use zoning elements such as the industrial estate and the embryo of neighbourhood planning.

Much of the best Garden City Architecture falls just outside the scope of the present view: the pre-1914 development was of a very high visual standard exploiting simple materials such as roughcast brickwork and tiled roofs to produce designs of an enduring freshness. In the inter-war period the originality and vigour of the originals tended to decline into stereotyped copies in both private and public sector and in the 1930s the evolution of international modern architecture passed the Garden City by.

The Cloisters
W H Cowlishaw
1906-8

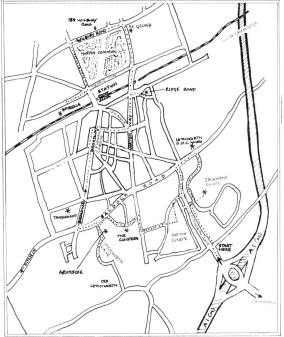

Tanglewood 17 Sollershott West
M H Baillie Scott
1907

Start of the A1(M) interchange with A6123. Letchworth Gate was originally laid out in 1931 as a parkway approach to the town from the old Great North Road to a landscape design by Barry Parker. At the junction with Baldock Lane the **Co-operative Dairy** (C F Moxom, 1935) is one of the few examples of mainstream, modern architecture of the 1930s, looking rather out of place like a pit-head bath (the architects were from Barnsley). Letchworth Gate is flanked by two examples of post-war mass housing: to the north the vast **Jackmans Estate** on Radburn principles of pedestrian/vehicular segregation (associated architects: William Barnes, Martin Priestman, Leonard Brown, 1960-73): to the south the **Lordship Estate** by Wates (Master Plan by Shankland, Cox) showing an equal lack of concern for the special Garden City character. Make a slight detour

Letchworth UDC housing
1921 (contemporary photograph)

northwards to **Jackmans Place** developed by Letchworth Urban District Council (Bennett and Bidwell), 1919-1921) which uses every trick in the book — the books being Raymond Unwin's *Town Planning in Practice* (1909), and the Unwin-influenced *Tudor Walters Report* (1918) which made Garden City standards mandatory in state-aided Local Authority housing. A longer detour southwards to the Glade, off Hitchin Road, will include **Hallbarn** by Robert Bennett (Bennett and Bidwell) the apotheosis of the Arts and Crafts house. Bennett, formerly an assistant of Parker and Unwin, used the Edwardian angled sun-trap plan, with free Tudor details, which recall his admiration for Baillie Scott: internally open-plan, inter-connecting rooms with superbly detailed inglenook fireplaces and joinery. Nearby in Letchworth Lane, **Dents Cottage** (Bennett and Bidwell, 1922) has picturesque, white roughcast walls and a red pantiled roof, a late example of the type which began with the nearby **Arunside** built 1904 by Parker and Unwin for their own occupation which acted as a prototype for many Garden City houses.

The central portion of Broadway (originally designated Town Square, now J F Kennedy Gardens) should have presented a visual climax to the Garden City with a complex of formally designed civic and religious buildings in the centre. It fails. A sketch design *modelled on the works of Wren and other masters* was produced in 1912 and the outline of the buildings was optimistically planted with Lombardy Poplars which still remain. At the south end **St Michael's Church** (Laurence King, 1966-69) is rather too small to make a visual impact but fits ingeniously onto its corner site, neatly detailed with brick screen walls in saw-toothed fashion containing glazing slits filled with excellent modern stained glass by John Hayward. The composition is surmounted by a cupola and spirelet. Running northwards along the western side of the square the former Grammar School (Barry Parker, 1931) presents a long unrelieved neo-Georgian facade whereas the **North Herts College** (County Architect, 1963) turns its back on the square. Moving eastwards across Broadway the **Town Hall** (Bennett and Bidwell, 1935) is dull neo-Georgian with a slight Colonial Williamsburg flavour opposite the timid moderne of the **Library** (C M Crickmer, 1938). Nearby on the corner of Gernon Road and Eastcheap **The Broadway Cinema** (Bennett and Bidwell, 1935) makes good use of patterned concrete blocks which frame the large intricately traceried windows.

Station Place Broadway
Garden City Corporation Offices
Barry Parker
1912
Foreground

North Herts DC

Only one company can claim to be 'The better brickmaker.'

Ibstock are the better brickmakers. Not only do they manufacture a range of over eighty premium facing bricks in a wide variety of colours, textures, types and sizes. Produce special shapes either to BS:4729 or exactly to a designer's specification. And offer interlocking coping and paving to withstand vehicular traffic. But their network of factories throughout the U.K. is supported by a full Design and Technical Advisory Service giving technical data, application details and expert advice on all brickwork questions.

OVER **80** BRICK TYPES

NEW INTERLOCKING COPING SYS...

SITE SERVICES

SAMPLE

IBSTOCK
THE BETTER BRICKMAKER

IBSTOCK, LEICESTER LE6 1HS. TELEPHONE IBSTOCK (0530) 60531.

From Gernon Road and Eastcheap, pedestrian ways run through to the town centre development (Damond Lock and Grabowski, Anthony Walker, 1971-75). The use of a rich red brick, tile hanging and tile canopied roofs obviously represent an attempt to integrate the development visually with the Garden City but fail to conceal the unrelieved blocks of supermarket and market hall. At the junction of Leys Avenue and Norton Way South is **The Free Church** (Barry Parker, 1923) with its Greek Cross plan and arcaded porch. Southwards along Norton Way to No. 296 — **The First Garden City Museum.** The earliest portion is a romantic re-creation of a thatched roofed Hall House, built in 1907 as the Letchworth offices of Barry Parker and Raymond Unwin. The two-storeyed central portion was added by Barry Parker in 1937 when the building became his home and he sensitively separated it from the original by a small gap to avoid disrupting the roof. Finally in 1977 a neatly detailed octagonal pavilion with a low-pitched slated roof was added (Letchworth Garden City Corporation, consultants: Architectural and Planning Partnership) which now contains a permanent exhibition devoted to the development of the First Garden City and the unique lifestyle of the pioneers. In the original building the large drawing office has now become an exhibition gallery but Parker's private office has been retained intact with its copper-hooded inglenook fireplace original fittings and sketches, vividly evoking the Arts and Crafts design theory which had been brilliantly extended from the smallest object to the community as a whole.

North of the railway in Bridge Road the Spirella factory is the most dominant building (C H Hignett, 1912-22) grouped around a landscaped courtyard. Visually the guilding represents a compromise between the Arts and Crafts movement reflected in the hipped roofed pavilions and a more frankly modern approach seen in the patent-glazed workshop wing. A pioneering example of reinforced concrete of the buildings, exposed beams in the workshops, with their segmental arches and glazed infill, strikingly anticipate a mid-century image: even the name of the building was cast into concrete. The vast scale of the building — *Castle Corset* makes the neatly detailed **Police Station** (Leonard Vincent and Raymond Gorbing, 1966-68) look puny by comparison. Nevells Road, site of some of the exhibits of the famous 1905 Cheap Cottages Exhibition, is worth a detour — along Cross Street, Icknield Way and the Quadrant to see some of the ingenious responses to the overall cost limits of the £150 cottage. One of the most noteworthy, No 4 **Cross Street** (Gilbert Fraser for the Concrete Machinery Company, Liverpool, 1905) is technologically interesting in that the walls were built from blocks made on site by a portable machine and won a special prize for the best concrete cottage.

St George, Norton Way North (Peter Bosanquet of Brett, Boyd and Bosanquet, 1961-64) has a downward sweeping roof of almost domestic scale contrasted to the tall concrete spire, formed of two sides of a triangle which encloses a rooflight and penetrates through the roof to serve as a backdrop for Altar and Crucifix. A final detour northwards to Wilbury Road will include two of the most revolutionary of the 1905 Cheap Cottage exhibits. No. 158 (J A Brodie, Liverpool City Engineer, 1905) was a prototype for a precast heavy panel prefabricated system and was manufactured in Liverpool complete with window frames, then dismantled and re-erected in the Garden City.

Mervyn Miller

Ridge Road

Spirella Factory
C H Hignett 1912-22

158 Wilbury Road
J A Brodie
1905
One of the prefabricated "cheap" cottages.

MOOR PARK

6 Temple Gardens
Connell Ward and Lucas
1936
The only example in this book of the houses by the pioneering firm Connell Ward & Lucas. Despite its splendid setting in the grounds of one of Hertfordshire's finest mansions, the house lacks the style of some of their other work: it is less clearly a unified whole. Part raised on piloti, it consists of a raised main floor, entered through a tall stair-tower projection. The dining room has a projecting curved bay, but this is unconvincingly in proportion to the whole. The various elements of the house have begun to separate themselves out as become the norm after the war. The pavilion for outdoor sleeping accommodation on the roof has been glazed.

NAST HYDE

Torilla Wilkins Green Lane
F R S Yorke
1935
An early house designed by the author of *The Modern House,* Torilla is a purist, two-storey house built with solid concrete walls, floors, and roof slab. The main stair rises out of the double-height living room, which is lit, in addition to its large picture windows, by a chequer board clerestorey. One of the few houses in Britain to approach the Continental, Cubist-inspired passion for interaction of planes, but is and looks, heavy upon the ground.

KNEBWORTH
Church of St Martin
London Road
Sir Edwin Lutyens
1914-15
with **Sir Albert Richardson,**
Houfe & Partners
1963-64
A grand, Tuscan church with startling brick quoins, whose construction was halted by the First World War. Finally completed in 1962 by Sir Albert Richardson.

Lutyens had a family connection with Knebworth, and also designed the *Golf Clubhouse, Homewood,* Deards End Lane, and three sets of cottages.

RADLETT

R Einzig

Skybreak House The Warren
Foster Associates
1966
An extremely early house by one of the best known British architects currently practising. The glazed south front is really a series of gables, and was clearly in advance of its time. The interior is very spacious. It is unlikely Foster would adopt the same techniques today. It is at right angles to the norm: three bays running downhill, separated with brick cross walls: each gable is glazed as are part of the roofs as they descend.

ST ALBANS

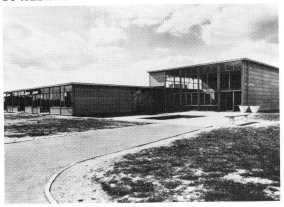

ROYSTON
Cottage Hospital London Road
Barry Parker
1924-28
A double 'Y' plan hospital, whose appearance lives up to its title. Note also: Old people's houses, Orchard Road, Royston. Paul Mauger (1945).

SAWBRIDGEWORTH
Bullfields
T F P Architects
1977
A modern re-creation of the terraced street, in two parallel rows. Simple colour washed brick walls and clay tiled roofs.

Margaret Wix School High Oaks
Architects Co-Partnership (M Cooke-Yarborough)
1954 C Miskin & Sons Ltd
One of over 40 schools designed by Architects Co-Partnership between 1949 and 1960, of which others in Hertfordshire include *High Oaks*, in St Albans (1954), *Oaklands Infants* in East Barnet (1951), *Park Lane Secondary* in Waltham Cross (1957) and *Burleigh Secondary School* in Hatfield (1956). It uses the typical 8-feet 3-inch module steel frame, with precast concrete panels. It was one of the first primary schools to be designed around a completely enclosed courtyard.

171

St Albans College of Further Education
Hatfield Road
Hertfordshire County Architect's Department
(J Wakely)
1958-60 William Sindall Ltd
Another building which demonstrated that with sensitivity the Hertfordshire steel frame system could be made to produce elegance. The College consists of a series of simple pavilions, linked to each other by elevated or ground-level corridors, well set into a sloping landscape with many mature trees. There are facilities for four main groups of subjects — commerce, engineering, crafts and domestic subjects together with specialist facilities for the integral College of Building. It is arguable that this system is best set off against a fine setting such as this: on a flat, featureless suburban landscape it would convey less pleasure. RIBA Bronze Medal 1959-60.

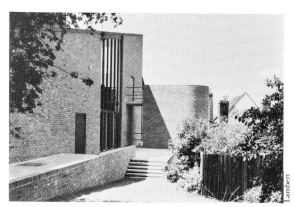

Lambert

St Albans School: Abbey Gateway
Sheppard Robson & Partners (I Goss)
1966-68
A delightful new hall on a restricted site, skilfully built into a hillside. Pleasant red-brown bricks, copper roof and dark stained windows. RIBA Award 1969. Civic Trust Commendation.

ST ALBANS

Seventh Day Adventist Church
Melvin Lansley Mark (D Brooke)
1981
Offspring from the Grove Hill Centre, containing other insignia of MLM work particularly in the heavy roof, and fascia to the flats behind.

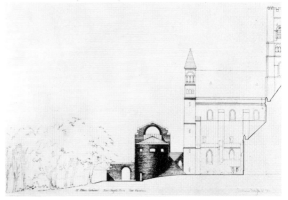

Chapter House, St Albans Cathedral
Whitfield Partners
1982
A curious post-modern building on the site of the ancient Chapter House and hence a source of controversy. The building will contain the choir school and other offices. This is an Italian conception in neat brick: it has an elegantly curved apse, and a bell tower on top. Extraordinary to find William Whitfield sufficiently unbending to permit such touches of historicism. It could become one of St Albans' most significant buildings.

STEVENAGE

Henry Moore Family Group
Barclay School

Barclay School Walkern Road
Yorke Rosenberg Mardall
1950-51 Gilbert Ash Ltd
The first co-educational Secondary Modern School in Hertfordshire, since adapted to take handicapped children. The school has the light spacious quality which became the accepted norm for Hertfordshire schools, and is notable as being an early building by Yorke Rosenberg & Mardall. As was fashionable there is a sculpture by Henry Moore, William Morris wallpaper in the dining room, and an abstract mural by Kenneth Rowntree. Architecturally, the building is in transition between the cubic volumetrics of the '30s and '50s featurelessness.

STEVENAGE

Stevenage was the first of the Greater London New Towns, visualised by Patrick Abercrombie's *Greater London Plan 1944,* and designated by central government under the New Towns Act, 1946. Conceived when Britain was under aerial bombardment in World War 2, the New Towns were planned to provide homes and employment for Londoners living and working in unsatisfactory surroundings, about 30 miles from the capital, and separated from it by open country.

Stevenage was originally intended to have a population of about 60,000 and was based on an existing community with a population of about 6,500. The designated area of some 6,250 acres is set in the attractive undulating Hertfordshire countryside, north of London and astride national road and rail routes between the capital and Scotland.

The elements of the Master Plan — residential neighbourhoods, employment areas, town centre, recreational areas and road framework are simply related and located to take advantage of the natural environment. There are two entrances to Stevenage from the A1(M) — a third is planned from a future east-west motorway — and these provide immediate access to all parts of the town. The railway and bus stations form an interchange at the heart of the Town Centre and Luton Airport is only 8 miles to the west.

By June 1980, when the population was about 73,000, the Development Corporation, the agency appointed under the New Towns Act to create the new town, had virtually completed its task and was wound up. Its housing stock of some 20,000 homes had been handed over to the Borough Council in 1978; in 1980 the remainder of its assets were handed over to the New Towns Commission.

Planning, designing, building and managing a successful new community involves many interests and dedicated work by many people. Those buildings listed can be but a typical selection from the very large number constructed in the period 1950-1980.

Many were designed in the Corporation's Department of Architecture and Planning, and it is unfortunately not possible within the compass of this guide to name all those who made their contribution to the Corporation's £100 million programmes of planning, acquisition, construction and landscaping.

Town Centre

Stevenage was the first of the New Towns to incorporate a fully pedestrianised shopping centre, following the precedent of the war-damaged cities of Coventry and Rotterdam. The first phase — Town Square, Queensway and Market Place — was opened formally by HM Queen Elizabeth II in 1959.

It gained a design award from the biennial Exposition of International Architecture at Sao Paulo in 1961.

Vincent, Gorbing

**Roebuck Gate
Broadwater**

This mixed housing development, which gained a Civic Trust Award in 1965, stands at one of the entrances to Broadwater Neighbourhood and complements the older group of buildings, including the historic 'Roebuck Inn', established at the junction of the former Great North Road and the Hertford Road.

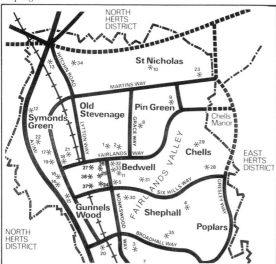

Vincent, Gorbing

Leisure Centre
Town Centre
Located in the Town Centre between the BR and Bus Stations, this building incorporates comprehensive provision for sport and the arts. Accommodation includes sports, practice and bowling halls, squash courts, conditioning and changing rooms, together with a 500-seat air-conditioned theatre/cinema, dressing and rehearsal rooms, scenery store and workshop. There are individual studios, an exhibition gallery, viewing areas, a creche, bars and a cafeteria.

Stone

Dixon's Warehouse
Pin Green
Vincent Gorbing & Partners
This building provides secure storage and service accommodation for photographic, audio and television equipment retailed by Dixon's chain of outlets. There is 13,500 m² of warehousing, 1,500 m² of equipment servicing, 830 m² of offices and 2,200 m² of ancillary accommodation; the building has been recently extended.

Those wishing to study the Stevenage story in more detail should refer to the Corporation's final publications 'Stevenage 78, Updating of the Master Plan: Written Statement' and 'First New Town', *An Autobiography of the Stevenage Development Corporation 1946-1980.*

Chief Architect-Planners, or Chief Architects
Clifford Holliday (1947-1952), Donald Reay (1952-1954), Leonard Vincent (1954-1962), Leslie Aked (1962-1979) and Brian Alford (1979-1980)

Some interesting schemes
HOUSING
Old Stevenage Flats, Sish Lane, 1952. Yorke, Rosenberg & Mardall.
Old Stevenage Houses, Trigg Terrace, 1952. SDC Architects' Department.
Broadwater Houses, Broad Oak Way, 1955. SDC Architects' Department.
Shephall Houses, Wigram Way, 1957. SDC Architects' Department.
Bedwell Flats and Houses, Penn Road, 1961. Brett, Boyd & Bosanquet.
Broadwater Flats and Houses, Roebuck Gate, 1963. SDC Architects' Department.
Broadwater Sheltered Housing, Shephall Lane, 1966. SDC Architects' Department.
Pin Green (Almond Spring) Houses and Flats, Grace Way, 1966. Vincent, Gorbing & Partners.
Pin Green (Sish's End) Houses, Verity Way, 1966. SDC Architects' Department.
Pin Green (St Nicholas) Houses, Ripon Road, 1970. Napper, Errington, Collerton & Associates.
Town Centre Flats, Silam Road, 1970. Vincent, Gorbing & Partners.
Symonds Green Houses, Shoreham Close, 1974. SDC Architects' Department.
Old Stevenage Houses, Barrow Court, 1980. Borough Technical Officer's Department, Stevenage Borough Council.

INDUSTRY
Industrial Area, Gunnels Wood
Electro Methods, Caxton Way (now Fleming Radio), 1953. SDC Architects' Department.
British Visqueen, Phase I, Six Hills Way (now ICI), 1955. SDC Architects' Department.
Kodak, Phase I, Caxton Way, 1956. SDC Architects' Department.
John Lewis Warehouse, Gunnels Wood Road, 1963. Yorke, Rosenberg & Mardall.
ICL, Phase I, Gunnels Wood Road, 1965. Oliver Carey.
Amoco, Gunnels Wood Road, 1968. Vincent, Gorbing & Partners.
Thermal Syndicate, Maxwell Road (now Taylor Instruments), 1970. K Barron.
Acton & Boorman, Cavendish Road, 1972. P E Williams.

Industrial Area, Pin Green
Dixon Photographic, Cartwright Road, 1974. Vincent, Gorbing & Partners.
Town Centre, Phase I, 1955. SDC Architects' Department.
Town Centre, Phase II, 1957. SDC Architects' Department.
Town Centre, Phase III, 1960. SDC Architects' Department.
Town Centre, Phase IV, 1965. SDC Architects' Department.
Chells, Elm Green Sub Centre, 1962. SDC Architects' Department.
Chells, The Glebe District Centre, 1966. SDC Architects' Department.

MISCELLANEOUS
The Twin Foxes Post House, Rockingham Way, Bedwell, 1953. SDC Architects' Department.
St Andrew's Church, Bedwell Crescent, 1954. SDC Architects' Department.
Swimming Pool, St George's Way, 1960. SDC Architects' Department.
Youth Centre, St George's Way, 1965. Vincent, Gorbing & Partners.
Leisure Centre, Lytton Way, 1975. Vincent, Gorbing & Partners.
Divisional Police HQ, Lytton Way, 1975. Clifford Culpin & Partners.

de Maré

FIRA Headquarters Gunnels Wood Road
Howell Killick Partridge Amis (A H Miller)
1965 Turriff Construction
The building provides for technical research by the
Furniture Industry Research Association, in an industrial estate in Stevenage. It is relatively rare for
an industrial building of this sort to choose architects
of the quality of HKPA, but FIRA had to deal with a
site that was slightly below ground level, and needed to
make an impact since it was adjacent to a main road.
Three wings of the building radiate from a main
entrance hall, which has a slightly brutalist feel about
it: various joints are bolted, visibly, and the way the
timber beams are supported by concrete columns is
reminiscent of nineteenth-century warehouses. Externally, the building is painted brick surmounted by
glazing.

Vincent, Gorbing

Homefield School Shephall Green
Hertfordshire County Architect's Department
(B Woodthorpe)
1976 Rayner & Bullen
A school for 90 severely handicapped children in a
conservation area fronting a village green within
Stevenage. Planned around an internal courtyard, the
school's interior is dominated by red brick, stained
timber walls and timber planked ceilings. The
dominant red pantiled roof, topped by a rooflight,
covers the main hall. More interesting inside than out.
Civic Trust Commendation 1978, RIBA Commendation 1978, School Design Commendation 1977.

Lister Hospital
North-West Hospital Board
Regional Architects
1972
A major regional hospital, acting as
a landmark for many miles. Its tall,
clean, white form was intended to
promote an image of health, and the
building has been designed for
expansion if necessary.

TEWIN

Village Green Housing
Adams Huntley Associates
1969-79
An example of 'vernacular' houses whose pitched roofs are carried down over the porch. A sensitive scheme, particularly in view of the fact it was designed for a builder. Civic Trust Commendation and DoE Award.

Sewell's Orchard
Mary Crowley
1936
A group of three bare brick houses for different members of the same family. Certain features — the mono-pitch roof with the rising eaves, the projecting gable and the fenestration — are those to be adopted post-Festival of Britain for houses in places ranging from Harlow to Glenrothes. The square chimneys are rather Mediterraneanish, and the boxed out windows an early appearance of this feature (original photograph).

TRING

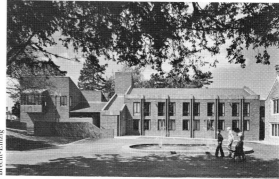

Brecht-Einzig

Offices, Vicarage and Church Hall
Melvin Lansley & Mark
1974
The conversion of the neo-Elizabethan, Victorian Vicarage as offices, linked to a new block of offices at right angles to it to form a courtyard, provided the opportunity to build both a new Parish Hall and a new Vicarage. The old Vicarage is sensitively restored, and the new offices complement it in a dark red brick and a neatly proportioned slate roof, and dark timber. The new Vicarage down the hill behind is a simple brick rectangle with an assertive, projecting, semi-circular staircase which lends a certain monumentality. The atmosphere of this development is its greatest asset: an atmosphere that combines English tradition (within the lee of the church) with modern building. RIBA Award 1975.

Tring Vicarage

Brecht-Einzig

Great West Plantation
Alan Tye
1976

A clean, Scandinavian, apparently flat-roofed building set into a hillside on the outskirts of Tring. It is T-shaped, the uphill wing being the office, whilst the stem and the downhill two-storey wing comprise the private house. The roof is laid on black stained tree trunks, which provides the necessary fall for rainwater as well as a startling visual contrast with the white walls. The main drawing room is double-height, facing south, with the kitchen projecting into it from the storey above. The designer is also the designer of Modric Ironmongery. RIBA Commendation 1977.

WESTMILL

The Rookery Aspenden Road
Bennett Howard King
1976

A small housing scheme in an outstanding village, combining old people's cottages and family houses. Landscaping by Preben Jacobsen is exceptional, and the colours of the brick and design of the enclosure are first class. The County Planning Department considered the scheme important in that it set a standard for new developments in sensitive areas. *The Rookery* was the successor to a proposal for undistinguished suburban sprawl on a different site.

WATFORD
Printing Works, Odhams
St Albans Road
Sir Owen Williams
1936
Yates Cooke & Derbyshire
1954

Williams' original facade was two-storey, built of brick and concrete with the water tank above the entrance. Its main interest lay in the structure of the main works floor, together with the plain glass and concrete design of the solvent recovery plant. The most prominent part of the development, however, is the main Press Hall which was designed by Yates, Cooke & Derbyshire in 1954. The clock tower is probably influenced by Stockholm Town Hall.

Hille's Headquarters
St Albans Road
Erno Goldfinger
1959-62

Goldfinger has not had the chance to build much in this country, and is notorious for the fine Alexander Fleming House, Elephant and Castle (South London) and his two gigantic housing developments in Poplar and North Kensington — both London. Note also offices in *Exchange Road, Watford*, Douglas Stephen and Partners (1965).

WELWYN GARDEN CITY

27-29 Handside Lane

100 Handside Lane

Welwyn Garden City, some distance from the old village of Welwyn (now somewhat engulfed by suburbia) was founded in 1920 by a private company under the influence of Ebenezer Howard. It had the opportunity to learn from Letchworth's mistakes. In April 1920 Louis de Soissons was appointed planner and company architect. By June he had presented the Directors with the first plan and work began almost immediately. De Soisson's background was the French aristocracy, and in central Welwyn there are echoes of Versailles.

The plan had a few main determinants: the railway, which bisected the city north and south; the industrial area adjacent to it; a 'central area' immediately to the west of it; and informal groupings of houses beyond.

The centre of the town is a formal neo-classical composition centred on the grand Boulevard Parkway with an apse at the top, called Campus, and an eastward link — Howardsgate — to the station. As such, it has a presence which renders it distinct from expanded villages, but not that much better than the grander shopping parades of North London. The materials are brick, stone dressings and neo-classical details. Howardsgate was originally designed to cross the railway lines to provide a proper eastern entrance to the Garden City. It foundered on objections from the Railway Companies.

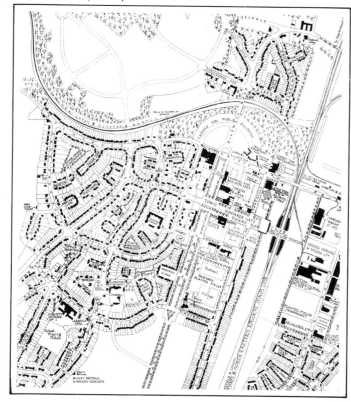

A progress plan of Welwyn by Louis de Soissons, 1936-7. The Roche complex is shown as playing fields and the modern houses kept severely north of the railway line.

Allen

Parkway

The earliest houses, **29-79 Handside Lane** (1920-21) were built by workers who were to construct the Garden City, whilst living in a hostel. The pitched roof, arched and rendered influence of Letchworth is clear which is curious in view of de Soisson's lack of enthusiasm for the place (the architects were C M Crickmer and A Foxley). He encouraged experimentation, one result of which can be seen in the quoined blockwork house at **100 Handside Lane** (1922), designed by L Martin.

The Quadrangle

Allen

Typical of the earlier work is de Soisson's **1 and 3 The Quadrangle** (1921), low-cost cottages with mansard, dominated by a carefully preserved tree; the neo-Wimbledonish **10, 11, 12 The Valley Green** (1921-25), by A W Kenyon; the **Norton factory** which is an American design for an American firm and was the second to be built in Welwyn, and the **Shredded Wheat Factory** which de Soissons designed with A W Kenyon in 1926.

Valley Green

Allen

In 1933, de Soissons and Kenyon designed a block of four speculative factory units in **Broadwater Road.** Although mutilated, the building could easily be restored, the metal glazing pars painted red, and the glass cleared. If so, the elegance and innovation of this symmetrical, curtain-walled building could be appreciated.

Of course, other architects were invited to participate. De Soissons, despite his revivalist preferences, was prepared to tolerate modern architecture, always as long as it created its own sense of grouping. Other houses of interest include **17 Sherrards Road,** by C H James (1933) who, with C M Hennell designed a number of buildings at Welwyn which Raymond McGrath thought to be *much of the best work at Welwyn*. The house is a curious mixture of a two-storey brick house, a steep-pitched roof containing a third storey, yet horizontally proportioned metal windows (Hennell worked at Silver End, Essex).

Broadwater Road Factories

Allen

180

2
Lanercost
Close
Mardley Hill

RIBA

Mauger and May designed a group of modern brick houses in **Pentley Park,** of which the proportions, and pleasing door and window details of No 26 (1937) should be noticed. E C Kaufman designed **24 Pentley Park** in 1938. In one of the outlying villages, Mardley Hill, Wells Coates placed a **Sunspan** bungalow at **2 Lanercost Close** in 1935. Although now much altered, this house is interesting as the only Eastern England example of Coates' prototype houses exhibited in Olympia in 1934. This exemplar was single storey (as compared to the grander two-storey version built in Angmering in 1936). The aim was a house whose internal planning could be changed effortlessly, but one which made best use of the sun. The plan, therefore, is L-shaped, with the entrance at the heel. The L is filled in with a rounded, south-facing living room, sandwiched between two wings containing all other rooms. It is built of dovetailed steel sheeting.

Roche Headquarters (right)
Broadwater Road

Potter

In 1939, Professor Otto Rudolph Salvisberg injected modernism with more than just a touch of Swiss anaesthesia into the industrial area with his **Roche Headquarters.** It is a very plain and pleasant L-shaped development of two and four-storey blocks of which the former — with its oversailing roof, piloti, and vertical mullions at the north gable, is the more striking. The glass-enclosed circular staircase is a gem.

POST-WAR WELWYN

In 1948, Welwyn became a New Town, linked to nearby Hatfield, under the Welwyn-Hatfield Development Corporation.

4 Ashley Close
William Allen
1948

This L-plan house, with a single-storey dining room projecting between the two arms, was the first in Britain with underfloor heating since Roman times. Clearly of its period — plain pitched roof, chimneys, windows, open staircase and Festival of Britain detailing. See also **8 Ashley Close** by William Allen and John Bickerdike — which has an interesting plan of a tapering central social area, through from living room to kitchen, with flanking service rooms with a first storey above the rear portion.

The Templewood School Pentley Park
Hertfordshire County Architect's Department
(Cleeve Barr)
1950 C Miskin & Sons Ltd

This is an early example of the internationally renowned Hertfordshire system-built schools, with a basic structure of a light steel frame on an 8-feet 3-inch grid. The exact position of the building was determined by three fine existing trees, and the site contrasts with many subsequent schools by being set in extremely pleasant landscape. Each classroom is a self-contained unit with its own store and cloakroom. There are similarities to the Ecole de Plein Air, 1936, by Beaudouin et Lods.

4 The Glade
Architects Co-operative
Partnership
1951

A large, plain brick house on a split level. Folding back French windows open the living room to the patio. There is a maverick arched window.

11 The Reddings
John Bickerdike
1955

Fairly up-market house of the time, with much more elegant sense of proportion than was then fashionable.

Westwood

Laboratories and Canteen for Roche
James Cubitt Fello Atkinson & Partners (P Gray, R Walton)
from 1963; building above **1978**

The new developments since the war have either to do with tasks relating to the bulk production of tablets from basic chemical constituents, subsequent semi-automatic packaging, or else staff amenity and new administration. The buildings derive their character principally from the cool, elegant lines, precise detailing, affluent materials, and contrasts between both colours, material, and solid and void. There is a clear development in these buildings toward distinguishing visually between the main part of the building and the services/staircase. The interior of the staircase in the canteen block is particularly fine.

Brecht-Einzig

House for Mr and Mrs Plant
14 New Road, Digswell
Melvin & Lansley (P Mark)
1972
An interesting, almost Austrian, house outside Welwyn, of mono-pitch roofs, orange stained timber-work — particularly fine in the first-floor balcony — and a purplish brick.

Snoek

Campus West
Sheppard Robson & Partners (D Nixon)
1974 M & O Foster

This Leisure and Amenity Centre, combined with the County Library, is the focal point for the town centre, offering a wide variety of cultural and recreational activities. There is a hall for dancing, civic functions and banquets; an auditorium seating 350; bars and dining facilities; a library and administrative offices. There is also a separate fully glazed exhibition hall. The building's orange-red brick and crisp detailing contrast with the more flabby neo-Georgian of the rest of the town centre. The crispness is accentuated by the bands of dark painted timber windows.

A Select Explanation of References

Barcelona Pavilion. German Exhibition building in the Barcelona Exhibition 1929 by Mies Van Der Rohe. An essay in uncluttered and free-flowing spaces. The pavilion was defined, not by walls or roof, but by the plinth on which it sat.

Brutalism. An ambiguous term of mixed parentage dating to the early 1950s. It has come to signify any of three things: architecture using naked, board-marked concrete (béton brut); or architecture in which the use of unadorned materials is paramount; or heavy, unfeeling, brutalising developments.

Corbusian. After the Swiss architect C-E Jeanneret nicknamed Le Corbusier (1887-1965).

Dudok. City Architect of Hilversum, Holland, between the Wars, whose geometrically brick Town Hall was amazingly influential in Britain. This architecture of an assemblage of chunky brick rectangles was as widespread in Britain as the *International Style.*

Farnsworth House. A Platonic ideal villa: in reality an expensive country house elevated above the Fox River flood plain in Illinois, U.S., designed by Mies Van Der Rohe.

GRP. Glass reinforced plastic: a material fashionable for the ease with which it can be moulded.

Holden, Charles. Architect of some spectacular London Transport Underground Stations between the Wars viz: Cockfosters and Arno's Grove.

International Style. A term invented by two Americans to describe the unifying style of building demonstrated by the 1927 Weissenhof housing estate in Stuttgart. It came to imply building using modern materials (steel or concrete), long strip windows, and a white facade. The inspiration was Cubist.

Modern Movement. Difficult to define, but usually associated with (a) a flat roof; and (b) the International style. After World War II, it meant anything that was not traditional.

Mies Van Der Rohe (Miesian). A German architect (1886-1969) exiled to America and responsible for the campus at the Illinois Institute of Technology (where he was professor), the Seagram building in New York and many other schemes. Originator of the aphorism of "less is more" or "almost nothing"; wherein is implied an architecture so refined as to be imperceptible.

Piloti Stilts: A modern version of columns without some of their subtleties.

Post-Modernism. A new title for a stream of architecture which has been developing since the 1930s. Generically speaking, it celebrates style in architecture, and a greater variety of visual experience than most modern buildings encourage.

Radburn. A method of housing development layout named after the location of its first experiment. The aim was to create traffic-free, and thereby safe, central areas by restricting cars, garaging and parking to the perimeter. In a distressing number of cases, the occupiers ceased to use their front doors (facing the traffic-free area) and elevated their back or kitchen doors to front-door status. The reason: it was the door nearest the garage.

Royal College of Physicians. An influential, late 1960s building by Denys Lasdun in London's Regent's Park.

Segal, Walter. Austrian-born British architect who has specialised in simple timber buildings which non-skilled people can erect themselves. Examples can be found near Bedford and Woodbridge.

Self-built. A term usually applied to houses. It does not imply independent magical motive force by the house's components qua *The Sorcerer's Apprentice.* It refers to houses constructed by the occupiers rather than by builders.

Team 10. The youthful British-dominated group formed from the "Congrès International d'Architecture Moderne" during the last four days of CIAM in the 1950s.

Vernacular. Literally, when applied to buildings, meaning "untutored", or non-intellectual, i.e. the style of local builders. It now means the grafting on to modern intellectual buildings some of the stylistic spoor of the untutored ancients: pitched, tiled roofs, swallows in eaves, etc.

Venturi, Robert. American architect who, in the 1960s, had the heresy to apply pitched roofs, pediments and other historic details to his buildings, and do so in an intellectual way. A precursor to post-Modernism.

Inter-War Chronological Index

Index of Architectural Offices

Index of Buildings